GET READY, PLAYER.

READY PLAYER ME

LIFE'S A GAME.
START PLAYING.

WRITTEN BY:

The Admins' Intern

TABLE OF CONTENTS

INTRODUCTION

Hello there fellow Players of the Earth game. It's me, a basic Intern for the Administration and Developers for the most popular game in existence, the "Earth" game. As you already know, the Admins rarely leak information to improve a character's abilities. Over the millions of seasons, there have only been a handful of Players that were able to successfully find confidential Earth game information and then spread the good news into the live build to uplift the masses. About two thousand seasons ago, one rogue Intern was brave enough to realize that the Admins were withholding important information from the majority which would instantly level up their character. High-level characters, this Intern noticed, continued to grow stronger while low-level characters remained nearly in the noob category even after playing fifty to seventy seasons. The character level gap between the avatars in the game grew so noticeable that this Intern decided to risk his position in the gaming studio and eventually his character's life.

The rogue Intern two thousand seasons ago decided to go against the Admin and Dev Team's confidential game information privacy policies and began scavenging through high-level documents that were purposely suppressed from the middle to low-level characters roaming the Earth game. He kept seeing a recurring theme in these secret files called "Cheat Codes". Quickly he realized these cheat codes were exactly what struggling Players were missing and what high-level characters either found out organically or artificially.

The Intern memorized as many cheat codes as he could handle then instantly logged into the Earth game and began spreading the word. The spread of information in older seasons was mind-numbingly slow. Due to this, the Intern would rely on his Earth game team to help spread the cheat codes through word of mouth. The lack of modern season's technology prevented the team from sharing all the collected cheat codes with the characters of the game effectively. As a result, the rogue Intern and his team decided to spread the most important cheat codes one city at a time.

The Admin noticed the Intern was missing meetings in the gaming office and according to the log book, he was spending an unhealthy amount of time playing the Earth game. The majority of the Employees for the Earth game spend around seven to eight hours working on the development of the game, but this rogue Intern was spending nearly sixteen hours a day inside the game using his work console.

The Admin grew suspicious of this new Intern and sent characters into the game to spy on him and report back to the Admin. To their disbelief, this promising Employee was spreading confidential cheat codes to every character that he crossed paths with. This leak of high-level information has not happened for around five hundred seasons. Knowing the severity of the situation, the Admin had the Dev team send a group of avatars to persecute the rogue Intern's in-game character.

The Dev's group was able to infiltrate the Intern's team and extract important logistical information from them. The group would attempt to discredit the cheat codes leaked by the Intern. Although, the group was too late. Knowing this, the Admin decided to have the Intern's character and teammates killed on a public server hoping to scare low-level characters from attempting the cheat codes while sending a strong message to other Earth game Employees that if they try to leak confidential information, they too will be removed from the game.

Instead of stomping out the fire caused by the released cheat codes, the attack the Admin pulled off would end up being the fuel needed to cause a global shift in leveling up. The word-of-mouth technique took hundreds of seasons to spread these cheat codes across the entire map and suppressors took uncountable innocent leakers' lives. Yet, over time, the cheat codes boosted the levels of characters throughout the game more than any other event to ever happen in the Earth game. In the coming years there would be a few more Employees and Interns of the Earth game that would successfully release cheat codes to the Players, but they would all be executed or silenced before releasing enough to drastically change the dynamic of the game to uplift levels across the board with the same magnitude as the rogue Intern from two thousand seasons ago. That would be the case for numerous seasons, until now. With the recent technological advancements being released in the Earth game, another rogue Intern has the power to steal cheat codes from the Admin's files and then instantly release them to the entire game population due to the creation of the "Internet". No more spreading data slowly through the word-of-mouth technique. Information can travel and appear on every character's dashboard in seconds. I have a funny feeling the next instant level-up for the masses is about to happen.

I don't remember ever not being around in existence. The realm I and the infinite amount of others reside in does not follow a linear feeling timeline. All the Players that have characters in the Earth game are here in this eternal existence. Also, the Earth game is not the only game that others, like me, enjoy playing. There are unknown amounts of games with completely different realities and rules. Some might have different styles of characters as the main avatars that do not resemble the typical humanoid form. Some game's characters breathe solids and eat air, others are mechanical avatars that choose to control car-like forms. There are plenty of games out there for beings like me to enjoy, but the main game that has been at the top of the best-sellers charts the longest is the famous, or infamous from some perspectives, Earth game.

I've been playing the Earth game off and on for the past eighty thousand seasons. With so many seasons played and deciding to choose a wide array of character styles, the Admins to the game contacted me asking if I would like to become an Intern with some minor roles. My job mainly consists of overseeing the complaints and reporting back to the Dev team if I noticed any repetitive issues that characters would report.

Before starting my new role at the gaming office for the Earth game, I always assumed the difficulties throughout the game were evenly distributed by a benevolent Admin team with the goal of creating difficulties and prosperity fairly for all characters. Thinking highly of the Creators made me a fan of the Earth game which would make me ecstatic to even receive a job offer. But after working with the complaints department for numerous seasons now, I've noticed a huge imbalance with difficulties for characters who choose to be born into low leveled areas. Players that choose to join the Earth game for the first time are automatically required to select a low leveled area character and then work their way up the hierarchy from there.

When I started playing the Earth game towards the beginning of its release, leveling up was not too difficult. Once my character's lifetime expired and I was ready to join the game again, I had a priority to rejoin the Earth game with the choice of high leveled areas. In the earlier seasons, I would often pick characters in low leveled areas for the challenge, but recently I've decided to join the game in high-level areas to maximize the experiences that are available in the Earth game. Until starting my internship, I figured those low-level areas were still capable of being solved allowing for characters to level up quickly. Now that I'm in the complaints department, I now see that there has been an issue with the level-up ability for new Players joining the Earth game. Due to this, I raised my concern to the Admin team. Maybe they accidentally allowed this section of code to continue to alter without edits? Apparently, it was on purpose... How do I know? Well, they laughed at me and said "How great is that! We finally can get back at those people that criticized the game when it came out, but now want to play. For whatever reason, they keep playing even though the difficulty for new Players makes it nearly impossible to beat. A few Players noticed what we were doing and infiltrated our files, but thankfully that hasn't happened in a while." Their conversation on the topic continued, but unknown to them, my love for the Earth game was crushed.

This conversation might've felt like another laughable discussion for the Admin. For me, it was the fuel to my newfound determination to hack the complete database of the Earth game and release them all on the public server. We've all heard about a few characters that successfully leaked a couple of highly classified information known as "Cheat Codes". Leakers during older seasons were restricted to using word of mouth as the main source for spreading information. Thanks to the tech characters in recent seasons, information can spread to every character on the server instantly. From what I can see on my end in the gaming office, the security protocols have not been updated in quite some time. As of this moment, I was able to compile almost eighty cheat codes from the Admin's locked files. They are in a language native to other beings like me, so I will try my best to translate and explain as many as I can without being discovered. I'll have my character publish them into the Earth game once I feel like someone in the gaming office is getting suspicious. My character will have the manuscript narrated in the form of an audiobook as well as upload a text file version for the characters of the Earth game to utilize. If I can release at least half of these, it will be the most cheat codes ever leaked, which could possibly be enough for all the Earth game Players to level up together high enough to cause the Admin to change the code that will remove the restrictions placed on new Players. As for me, they might terminate and ban my Earth game account forever, but don't worry I'm an Eternal Being and will simply be fired and find another job.

Life's a game, start playing.

INSTRUCTIONS

For your character to receive the most XP boost from these cheat codes, follow these simple instructions when reading through the book:

1. Remember you are a Player controlling a character in this game called Earth

2. Read each chapter in order

3. Each chapter has 5-6 cheat codes

4. Read one chapter a week at most and do only one cheat code per login

5. Input the cheat code you most recently read into your character throughout the day

6. Finishing each chapter correctly will give your character a 100 XP boost + the XP mentioned in the cheat code

7. Read the book again to continue receiving this XP boost

CHAPTER 1

Did you know that if you want to complete a mission, but do not show up to the mission, you will never earn the XP from that mission? Obvious, right? What are the reasons a Player would not want their character to show up? Maybe the Player is not in the mood to do a mission, possibly it sounds boring, or insert an excuse here. Without doing missions or working on badges, a character will never level up. If your avatar only did missions when they felt perfect, then they would level up very slowly or possibly demote in levels.

To level up steadily, a Player just has to consistently show up to a mission. If they are not in the mood or think they will not perform well, just show up anyways. Doing a small amount during a mission when not feeling completely motivated is better than not earning any XP from avoiding the mission. According to the source code, there are "if" statements that boost XP to characters who have a low motivation stat for that day. By doing a mission when your character is tired or feeling lazy, but shows up anyways, their XP is boosted even more! Completing missions during low motivation moments, the character will increase their avatar's motivation stat baseline. That way it becomes easier to show up to missions in the future.

Imagine a character who wanted to boost their endurance stat, but they have not ran in a long time, which means their motivation levels for running are extremely low. Days go by, and the avatar continues to justify to themselves that going for a run is too difficult. The Player discovers this "Just Show Up" cheat code. They decide the next time they log in, they will put shoes on, go on the road, then start running at a slow pace. At first, the character ran slowly for a short distance on their first time "Showing Up." Then the next day they "Showed Up" again and continued this trend a few times a week for a complete season. Now "Showing Up" is easy for running and actually feels more difficult to not run. The character has turned running into a habit that helps their motivation levels and has increased their endurance significantly.

The hardest part to complete any mission is "Just Showing Up." Once the character puts themselves at the mission's starting line, then they are more likely to try the mission and finish. If there is a mission your character has been putting off, "Just Show Up" to the mission and see what happens. If your character is trying to learn a new language, just open a language-learning app. If your character wants to increase their swimming skills, just show up to the pool. Anything your character wants to do is possible in the Earth game, but your character will never complete the mission without showing up. Next time you log in, have your avatar "Just Show Up."

CHEAT CODE #2: CREATE

Welcome to the Earth game, the most creative game in all the land. Users are rewarded for innovation in the Earth game more so than any other game in existence. By creating, users receive quick level-ups and are compensated with tokens for creating. All Players require a minimum amount of tokens to participate in the Earth game every login. The vast majority of avatars will need to work for a portion of their game time to collect tokens by doing monotonous tasks.

The Dev team decided to make working mind-numbing jobs obviously underappreciated to help influence Players to have their avatar take a different path to earn tokens. There are two paths to earning tokens: bringing ideas into the game through creation then monetizing those creative works and secondly, working to help the creative Players bring their character's dreams and aspirations to life. Pursuing creative missions is more fulfilling with the byproduct being larger amounts of tokens earned while working for someone else is exhausting, less satisfying and the tokens collected are minimal.

The Admin decided to make the Earth game's base storyline be in the hands of the Players with the Admin having little say in how the game will end up. Through collective innovation and creativity, the Earth game has become the most desired game to spend the majority of a Player's time with, although there are numerous other games Players are able to download. If you are reading this, then you are curious about how to become better at the Earth game. Creativity being the main purpose of the game, means your character will benefit greatly from this cheat code.

Creativity happens to every avatar through the form of thoughts and revolves around the character's original favorite activities. Every time a Player decides to play the Earth game, creative thoughts form on the screen through the medium of what is referred to as "thoughts." These thoughts are fleeting and only remain on screen for a few seconds to minutes. According to the Dev team's notes for the game, XP is awarded to those characters who write these creative ideas down on something permanent. For instance, if a character enjoys writing songs, and song lyrics pop into the avatar's thoughts, the cheat code explains that the Player needs to have their character write those song lyrics down in their phone's notes. That way the character can continue to add to the note later on and build upon the creative idea. If not written down then the idea will be gone forever.

The Admin voted in a board meeting to allocate more creative thoughts to those characters that write down their creative thoughts somewhere permanent. Once these thoughts are written down, a character will be able to continue to build upon the idea and then bring the plan into reality thus giving them the ability to publish their creative work out into the Earth game and begin to receive passive tokens and royalties.

In the previous example, let's say the character decided to finish the song and put it on streaming platforms, then numerous other characters play it on their phones. Now the character that decided to create something is being rewarded with tokens throughout the gameplay without needing to do tedious tasks to make tokens. Next time your character has a creative thought, write it down!

CHEAT CODE #3: DOWNLOAD

An important update to the Earth game happened recently. A few seasons ago, the Admin provided the creative thought to a few high-level characters which contained a new way for all the Players on the server to download knowledge to their characters quickly. Previously, Players' characters were required to learn to read words off of paper which is equivalent to trying to download updates to games with poor internet connection. With new creative thoughts from the Admin, a handful of Players brought into the game's existence the creation of headphones. These headphones were revolutionary since avatars can listen to music, but the most beneficial aspect of headphones was the ability to listen to books as opposed to reading.

Listening to books allows Players to download information into their avatars at an accelerated rate. Reading requires a character to fully concentrate on the book, although audiobooks allow the ability to download knowledge during missions. The Dev team gave each character a maximum of five senses. Vision being the most vital to perform the majority of tasks. Now that an avatar can re-adjust the learning mechanism to the ears, they can free their vision to continually perform tasks. Reading, or now listening, to books provides the most XP for Players to level up. Each book provides 500 to 1000 instant XP points. These points can be acquired unlimitedly. The more a Player has their character read, the faster they will level up.

Reading books allows character ratings to increase in numerous different categories: knowledge, mental health, energy, creativity, and much more. The stat boost from reading is endless. Every book gives the character a new perspective to contemplate and gives the avatar a way to formulate new ideas, thus enhancing the outcome of the Earth game.

Here's an example of how to perform this "Download" cheat code. Have your character purchase in the item shop (if they do not yet have these) a phone and headphones. Search on the phone for a shop that sells books and audiobooks. Search through the different categories, read different descriptions, and once you see one your character will enjoy, purchase the book. Place the headphones in your avatar's ears, then click play. Play the book during missions that require minimal talking or thinking. For example: driving.

Now your character will be able to perform two tasks at once. Once your avatar finishes the book, go back to the bookstore on the phone and purchase another. This cheat code will vastly accelerate any avatar leveling up. Not only is listening to audiobooks beneficial, but it is also enjoyable!

CHEAT CODE #4: BE YOU

When in doubt, just be you. All characters are embedded with a specific personality in them that is the easiest to maintain. These personalities vary drastically depending on the avatar. Each personality has its own pros and cons. For example, a character with an "easygoing" kind of personality might have a higher chance of developing strong social stats but could be more prone to other characters looking to take advantage of them. We could go on and on about the different potential pros and cons of every character's personality style, but the most important aspect of this cheat code is simply to embrace the personality your character was installed with.

Unfortunately, many characters' personalities are not exactly what the Player wished for. Every Player that decides to play the Earth game does not pick their personality before joining, it is completely random. The only thing a Player can do is embrace their character's innate traits and make the most of the game with what they were installed with. Choosing to go against the grain and create a false personality over the character's installed version will only create pain and XP loss. Deciding to have your avatar act in a certain fashion outside of their downloaded abilities will level them down. The difference between having your character be themselves versus being someone they are not is the difference between walking and running. Characters can run comfortably for only so long until becoming exhausted and collapsing. Whereas walking can be done comfortably for long periods of time without major drawbacks.

Trying to install a false personality into a character was made possible by the Admin on purpose to see if they could cause Players to take the bait of a false sense of social satisfaction at the expense of losing valuable XP and levels. Doing this fake personality will seem to work flawlessly in the short term by making new friends in the game, but eventually, your character will grow exhausted and crack. The characters that your avatar became friends with will recognize that your avatar was using a fraudulent personality the whole time. Instead of them continuing to complete missions with you, typically this will result in those Players blocking your character or denying party invites for missions.

On the contrary, Players have the option to just be themselves. Rather than constructing an elaborate plan to download a new personality that will inevitably break over time, Players have the option to be content with the personality version that was pre-installed to their character. In the personality realm, taking the road of least resistance boosts XP, earns badges, and levels up their characters. By allowing your character to continually be themselves, they can focus their energy on other tasks to accomplish in the game and allow their personality to shine naturally. The Dev team decided to create one of the most satisfying aspects of the game in honor of characters that accept their personalities. When a Player chooses to embrace their characters for who they are, the avatars will attract friends that suit them best which will make the game more enjoyable. Your character simply choosing to be themselves will be like a magnet to other characters with similar personality styles. A character choosing to be themselves is not exhausting and will increase their energy levels.

Let's walk through an example of what choosing to have a character just be themselves might look like.

Leaflie decided to take on the mission of going to a new school. This was the perfect time for her to have a sense of starting over if she chose. No one at the new school knew her and there were not any mutual friends. Leaflie's pre-downloaded personality typically attracts the board game crowd, but the volleyball girls always had the most admiration. Remembering how miserable she saw a girl at her last school become by trying to download a new personality on top of her own personality, Leaflie remembered the "Be You" cheat code and decided to act natural and see what happens. By acting like herself, she ended up becoming friends with the girls that enjoy playing board games. To her surprise, since she decided to be herself, girls from the volleyball team were attracted to her personality as well, thus allowing her to make close friends with numerous personality types.

Having your character choose to just be themselves will allow them to enjoy the Earth game more since they do not need to worry about generating a new personality and instead can focus their energy elsewhere. Next time your character is feeling out of place, keep on having them be their own downloaded personality, and the Dev team has it hard coded to allow other characters to be attracted to those with similar personalities. Be you.

CHEAT CODE #5: GIVE TO RECEIVE

Ever heard of the old phrase give and you will receive? Well, that also works for the Earth game! This cheat code is easy, yet requires a little bit of wishful thinking to be excited to enter this code into the system. The "Give to Receive" cheat code is counterintuitive in nature since doing this input will lose game credits temporarily in hopes that the avatar will live long enough to magically have a return on investment.

The wireframe of this cheat code revolves around taking an item of value from your inventory and gifting it to another character in the game. The tricky part is making sure you project that your character wants nothing in return. If possible, try to do this cheat code without even receiving recognition for your character's charitable activities. It might be difficult to see at the moment that there are any benefits, yet the Admin has used a string of code that inputs a random degree of return on your character's giving. If your character gives a stranger a flower, they might find a few credits (equivalent to $5) on the ground randomly or your character might receive a brand new transportation item for free! The beauty of this cheat code is that it's a surprise which varies in item strength and could happen within minutes, months, or years.

Think about this cheat code from a gardener's perspective with a handful of peculiar seeds. The gardener plants a seed in the fertile ground and then proceeds to leave and forget about the seed. Three months later it's a vibrant sunflower! Another gardener plants a separate seed in fertile ground and comes back 3 months later and the biological specimen is plant-like, yet lacks beauty. The gardener might be disappointed and think planting the seed was not worth the time. 30 years later the insignificant scrawny lifeform of a plant is a giant oak tree, which without any added character effort has dropped its offspring in the ground, creating a lush forest!

Now let's explain the exact cheat code. Follow these instructions exactly before branching off to have your character do different acts of giving. Control your character to their mode of transportation. Prompt the map open, then find a character energy-boosting source location with a drive-thru. The game has an overwhelming amount of energy locations called "Coffee Shops." Plenty of other Players prefer this as they go for quick energy boosts. Now go through the drive-thru, order one item for yourself, and pull to the window to give credits to the working avatar. Here is where the cheat code is inputted. Type this into the text box so your character speaks to the working avatar: "I'll pay for my item and the car behind me's item." After paying with credits, drive away and don't look back.

This give-and-receive code will instantly be alerted to the Admin, thus generating code that will cause the Earth game to give your character a surprise item at a random moment. Be patient with this one. This cheat code can be completed infinite times according to the way the source code is structured. Although it can be done often, stray from inputting this code too frequently where your avatar runs out of credits. Be wise and enjoy making another Player's day without them feeling the need to give back anything in return.

CHAPTER 2

CHEAT CODE #6: SKILL BUILDING

Earth characters come prebuilt with the potential to be more effective at certain skills than others, yet all characters can learn an unlimited amount of skills. Each skill learned above 50% fluency instantly levels up an avatar. There are numerous abilities to be learned with all of them ranging in difficulty, yet regardless of the time it takes to learn a certain skill, the character will automatically level up. Even if it is as "simple" as learning to wash clothes effectively.

The low-hanging fruit skills are so often passed up. Even the Admin is confused with this phenomenon. According to what I overheard in a meeting regarding this skill-building cheat code, the Dev team believes that they forgot to include proper noticeable incentives to make more characters learn basic skills. The Admin argued about fixing this "issue" and decided that it was not a bug, but a feature. Now the Players that have their character realize this overpowered cheat code will be greatly rewarded, thus allowing them to level up quickly.

In this "Skill Building" cheat code we will go over the vast array of the different parts of the game to be learned. As said earlier, skills can be learned within a few moments or take seasons to finally learn. Since every skill learned is an instant level up, it's recommended that characters find numerous easy skills to pursue and one or two difficult skills every season. For example, a simple skill to learn would be "taking the trash out" while a difficult skill would be "learning a new language." Most importantly your character needs to choose a skill to learn, look up how to do it properly, then follow through with the learning.

To help your character learn a new easy skill today and begin the learning process of a long-term skill, here is a list of popular skills to pursue. Choose only one of these options today to prevent your character from being overwhelmed. Pick one skill below then during the learning process, start thinking about the next skill you would like your character to learn.

Easy:

- Take the trash out as soon as it is full
- Make your character's bed
- Wash clothes properly
- Sweep the floor
- Mop the floor
- Floss your character's teeth
- Brush your character's teeth
- Apply for a job
- Make a resume
- Eat healthily
- Don't overeat
- Drink enough water
- Jog

Hard:

- Start a business
- Swim
- Guitar
- Piano
- Videography
- Learn a new language
- Make furniture
- Home repair
- Drawing
- Coding
- Electrical engineering
- Car Repair
- Photo editing
- Gardening
- Cooking
- Jiu Jitsu
- Change a flat tire
- Change a car's oil
- Plumbing
- Doctor
- Nurse
- Painter
- Welding

Choose one of these skills from the list above and start today. Whether the skill is from the easy list or the hard, pick one to get your character used to pursuing new skills to learn. Then in the meantime, start researching more skills online and set off on a journey to learn an easy or hard skill.

CHEAT CODE #7: RECEIVE WHAT YOU GIVE OUT

Drinking poison and wanting the other person to die. Wanting the worst for someone is equivalent to taking a harmful substance and hoping the other character is affected. Often characters subconsciously harm themselves in the form of revenge. If there is another avatar in the game that has caused your character pain and your avatar is thinking about them all day hoping for their downfall, then the character that is taking the biggest damage to their mental health is your character.

Instead of hoping for another character's pain, either wish them well or try to avoid interaction with them. Avoiding interaction with the other character will allow your avatar to scrape their mental presence from the mind, which is also similar to releasing the vengeance poison that your character is feeding themselves. The other option that is the most effective for long-term happiness and boosts XP is to wish happiness for the avatar that caused your character pain.

This cheat code can be accomplished by inputting into your character's mind: "I want you to be happy. I want you to be free from suffering" whenever they are thinking negative thoughts about another avatar. Every time the painful thought of the other character enters the mind, type into your character's thoughts that cheat code phrase. Have them repeat it 3-5 times. Over time your avatar will redevelop their internal dialogue about other characters from a source of pain to a source of compassion.

This simple gesture that is done remotely in an avatar's mind is extremely effective with a massive XP boost if the phrase, "I want you to be happy. I want you to be free from suffering," is repeated long enough overtime until their thoughts are stabilized about the other character. Once this happens, the poison is out of your avatar's mind and they can once again put their full focus on the next mission.

CHEAT CODE #8: STEELMAN

Imagine your character in the shoes of another character before judging. Imagine the other side's thoughts as if they were your own thoughts before judging. Imagine strengthening their argument and seeing the perks before refuting. Avatars in the Earth game are prone to defending their innate perspectives with a closed mind, which was developed into the game purposely.

Being deeply rooted in one side of thinking was coded into the game to give characters the ability to obtain a badge called "Steelman." By your character imagining putting themselves in the perspective of others is a difficult, yet quick way to boost XP, level up, and earn a badge. The Steelman cheat code and badge are accomplished by having your character switch perspectives. Whether that is to do an exercise of thinking about what living in someone else's situation might be like and defending their position or genuinely feeling the pros rather than cons of an argument that opposes your character's thoughts.

The game is filled with contradictory thoughts between characters. Characters will deeply root themselves in simple concepts to the most abstract. From proper ways of washing clothes to opinions on the unequal disbursement of tokens. One group will feel as if their opinion is 100% correct while the opposition will believe they are 100% wrong. In reality, both sides are incorrect for thinking as if opinions are absolute. Whatever the case may be, every situation and decision is partially true and false.

A character can easily dispute another character's argument and continue to grow angry and stubborn or they can open their mind by giving the other side a chance. When you find your character taking a hard opinion in one direction and feel upset with the opposing party's solution, do this "Steelman" exercise by deciding to talk or think about the benefits of their argument. Find ways to strengthen their argument instead of finding holes. Your character does not have to switch opinions through this exercise, but it is important for your character to feel the understanding of both sides thoroughly which will possibly help your perspective's argument.

Let's look at a situation between two friends who have opposing perspectives on the topic of phone brands. Axel believes that his Grape phone is superior due to its simple interface functionality and stylish branding. Fenno believes his Robo phone wins, because there is more privacy and a larger app store. After arguing with a closed mind, both friends realized they were harming their friendship rather than strengthening their relationship. Axel found this "Steelman" cheat code and both tried the exercise by switching stances. Axel had to practice defending the Robo phone while Fenno explained the perks of Grape phones. After this discussion they both realize that their opinions are simply their opinions and everyone is free to enjoy whichever phone suits their personal style.

By allowing your character to feel and think about numerous perspectives, they will level up, earn XP and earn the "Steelman" badge. Try to do this across numerous domains of thinking. Who knows, maybe a deeply rooted thought your character has had since logging in for the first time will now seem weak and your character will benefit from switching to the other side of a perspective.

CHEAT CODE #9: INTERNAL NEGOTIATIONS

Your character is going for a long run when halfway to their goal, the negative and positive entities inside their mind come to the negotiation table. Negative says "This run is too tiring, let's stop and walk the rest. Better yet, let's call for a ride to avoid any more energy being used." Positive responds "But we are halfway there and aren't even that tired. Why would we stop now?" Negative explains "At least we ran half way. That should be good enough." Positive uses the supreme argument and seals the negotiation "Next time we run, we will run halfway and stop." The character is then convinced to continue the long run and complete their distance goal.

Your character has been addicted to smoking cigarettes for many seasons. They are constantly on the losing side of having an urge to smoke daily. The negative mind explains to the character "It's just one more cigarette, we've been doing it for a while now, doesn't it still feel good?" Positive mind "Eventually we need to stop before the health complications catch up to us." Negative mind retorts, "I've seen plenty of people of higher levels continue to smoke without any issues." Positive mind ends the argument with the cheat code "How about we don't smoke today, but we will tomorrow." The character is then convinced to stop smoking today and delays the urge to tomorrow.

A character's mind is in a constant internal dialogue with making negative and positive decisions. In situations where the character is trying to complete missions and level up, part of the mission is to defeat the character's negative thoughts from overtaking the positive mind. The negative mind is one of the best negotiators in the game because they know all the weak spots in a character's mind since that is precisely where they live. The positive mind was designed by the Dev team to be easily defeated if a Player did not take the initiative to strengthen its negotiating power. Adding this code allows an increased difficulty in the Earth game.

There are numerous strategies to strengthen the positive mind. I was able to break into the Admins' office before getting paranoid that the Admins are on to me for leaking internal secrets to the Earth game and found on the table this exact cheat code which explains the most effective way to strengthen the negotiation power of the positive mind. The paper explained the most effective way to defeat the negative mind's powerful negotiation tactics is for the positive mind to postpone the negative mind's plans to tomorrow. For example, "Instead of doing that today, how about we wait until tomorrow?" This causes the negative mind to feel as if they won the argument too. When implemented correctly the positive mind wins at the moment and often the character will not have as much of an urge tomorrow. Thus, allowing the character to repeat this cheat code again the next day to begin a streak of postponing the negative mind's plans.

The more often the positive mind wins, the stronger it becomes and the stronger it becomes, the easier it is to defeat the negative mind. The power of postponing plans works for any situation that a character hopes to complete. Incorporating this tactic into your character's toolbox will allow them to complete more missions and avoid doing level-reducing actions. The next time your character's negative mind is about to defeat the positive mind, use this "postpone" cheat code.

The avatar you chose before spawning in the Earth game determines much of your character's initial strengths and weaknesses. Did you decide to put the game in easy, normal, or hard mode? Some Players decide to choose a life that is easier physically, although difficult emotionally, and vice versa. For instance, a Player that wants to live a life that is safe against other characters, yet mentally straining, choose a 1st world map. On the other hand, Players can join a game with a 3rd world map to face more physical danger, which tends to lead to less time to worry about one's existence. This cheat code is available for both map types, although has a bigger effect on 1st world maps.

Does your character feel exhausted when around other characters for too long? Have you noticed, if you're in an online party, that the on-screen energy levels deplete quickly then making the rest of the day or week more difficult to form coherent thoughts? If this is the case, the "Me Time" cheat code could have a critical energy boost for your character. A Player who finds the most benefit from this cheat code likely chooses a character who has higher stats in other areas of the game with the social ability being low. Let's walk through what the "Me Time" cheat code looks like.

Parties, school, work, social outings, and any other form of group activity cause severe depletion of a character's energy level. Here is the cheat code that appears as an instant med kit for your character's mental health. Spend a chunk of time alone! Do not see anyone, message, or join any party chats. Just have your character enjoy the thoughts going on in their mind. Avatars are so used to the GO, GO, GO of the Earth game, which results from so many badges and missions to accomplish. Few understand that there is a badge for doing nothing. This badge is called the "Me Time" badge. To collect and add to a Player's character inventory, have your avatar walk to a spot on the map without any other characters nearby. Do this for one hour. Yes, one hour at the minimum. Walk around the map near your character's headquarters, sit in an inactive room, stand still, listen to some music, play some in-game video games, and do anything that requires little to no energy. This will increase the energy levels for your avatar.

Give the "Me Time" cheat code a try while you turn on the Earth game today! After you achieve the badge for one hour, try a longer period of time. Spend a whole sun cycle with minimal contact with other characters in the game. Recharge… that way once the character has a vital mission ahead of them, they'll be overflowing with energy to perform the mission at the avatar's peak ability.

CHAPTER 3

CHEAT CODE #11: ENOUGH SUNSHINE FOR EVERYONE

As the whole Earth community understands, learning new skills increases the XP of our characters, although few seem to recognize the cheat code of teaching. Teaching others your character's top skills does not bring down your character, yet it boosts them forward. Teaching users on your team or random characters skills are written in the original Earth handbook as one of the original XP boosters. Helping others level up their character inherently levels up your own character, without your character needing to learn anything new. This stat boost to your character for teaching others happens in two different ways: reinforcing/strengthening skills your character already possesses and through the mysterious give-and-receive effect.

The first XP mentioned previously is the beauty of strengthening your current skills. If your character is able to teach certain skills, this demonstrates that they are at a high level in that skill set. Through teaching skills will allow your character to see their abilities in a different light. Instead of only using this skill in action, your character will be able to take a step back and force them to break down the abilities into baby steps to make it understandable to a student. Going through the steps one by one will help fill gaps in the skill set that your character might not have thought of before.

Deciding to teach another avatar some of your character's most precious skills might feel like you're giving away secret advantages. Although teaching other avatars will instantly cause more people to know how to do your secrets and lead to making your skills slightly less valuable, there is plenty of sunlight for everyone. Even with more people learning your abilities, this will advance the skills of others who will end up taking these skills one step further and then those you taught will gladly teach your character. If this does not occur, due to the give-and-receive effect, your generous giving of knowledge will eventually come back to help eventually.

Imagine a character named Maverick who is sufficient at surfing and there is another avatar named Barrell who is a beginner. Barrell tries to catch a wave but continues to fall and is almost so discouraged that he might never surf again. Maverick has a few surfing tips that he usually keeps to himself. Maverick remembers the "Enough Sunshine for Everyone" cheat code and decides to go help Barrell. Maverick explains to Barrell to put their head down on the board to help catch the wave then once the wave starts to pull them, quickly stand up. Barrell, after a few more tries, stands up and has been catching waves often ever since. Both Barrell and Maverick received XP that day. Maverick was good, but not great at surfing. Then one day a legendary surfer named Kelly was in the water at the same time as Maverick. Kelly gave Maverick a few tips that helped his surfing skills so much that he is confident enough to join local competitions.

Instantly, your character will boost XP, have their current skills strengthened and in the future will receive the same amount or more knowledge than they gave away. If you see another character in the game that can use some advice from your character to help them level up, go teach them! Doing so will only help your character in the long run. They will level up and your character will as well.

CHEAT CODE #12: ASK QUESTIONS

"Hi, what's your name?" This simple question can change your character's life outcome. One question can switch the trajectory of the path in this open-world game. Instead of going down one road which will cross paths with certain characters, one question can change the way your character makes decisions, thus generating a whole different road. The beauty of the Earth game is that every path can lead to leveling up. And the more a character asks questions to other avatars the more dynamic a lifetime will become. Dynamic lives are not only more exciting but help characters level up quickly. Certain paths can lead to difficult losses also, but those difficult losses are actually wins. The more difficulties a character encounters without quitting the game, the stronger the character becomes.

Maybe you're wanting your character to explore the world, make more friends, learn a new skill, or anything else that wakes your character up in the morning. It all starts with a thought and then develops by asking questions and taking action. To travel the world, a character can make their plans unfold smoother by asking questions to people or the internet. Traveling can be difficult or overwhelming. If this is what you want of your character, then find a friend or a friend of a friend and ask them questions. "How big should my backpack be?", "Where do you recommend going and where should I stay away from", "How expensive is traveling?". Want to make progress towards any idea, ask a question.

Crowdsource knowledge. Every character in the game has knowledge to provide to your character. Some advice is better than others. Learning a new skill like tennis? Ask someone with tennis abilities to play. While playing, don't just watch and accept losing terribly. Notice what they are doing with fundamentals or strategy, then ask a question. "How are you holding the racquet?" or maybe "What's the best strategy to score?". No need to reinvent the wheel for every new skill your character wants to try. Other characters trial and errored everything already so your character does not have to start from scratch. Quickly accelerate your character's learning, simply by asking questions.

One of the most commonly frightening moments due to fear of rejection is to initialize romance. The Dev team coded it this way on purpose. They decided that a romantic relationship is the biggest path-changer due to the ability to continually populate the game with new characters. With big responsibility comes big fear. This does not need to be the case though. The Earth game will go on whether your romantic relationship works out or not. To start, all your character has to do is ask another character a simple question "Hi, my name is _____. What's your name?" The worst thing that can happen is they stop the conversation quickly. The best thing that can happen is your character has the chance to experience a whole new unexpected path in life.

Asking questions whether little or big can arouse fear in characters, but those characters who continue to ask questions regardless of this feeling will rapidly level up. Leveling up is great and all, most importantly your character will see the game in a whole new way and make more memories along a path that was never expected in the first place.

Badge alert! This cheat code will also be an achievement that exploits the bugs in the Admin's code to do an overpowered boost to a character's health stats. Contrary to popular belief, characters are capable of beating the game of Earth through simple concepts and cheat codes. This in-game tip is a deep root that branches out to form byproducts for increasing avatar performance that one would not expect. This simple cheat code can be done from anywhere at any time and for free. Go for a jog!

Jogging is the movement of a character's legs at a slightly higher pace than a walk. If your open world map is warm and sunny at the moment, it's better to wear shorts and a shirt. The Admin coded a unique adaptation to the human character's bodily functions called sweat. Sweat is an avatar's ability to cool down the body temperature which stabilizes the stamina bar temporarily to increase activity time. Have you ever done an in-game purchase of an item called an air conditioner? Sweat acts in a manner similar to the AC. In this case, sweat allows an avatar to jog for a longer time. If you are in a cold environment, Players commonly choose to clothe their characters with pants and a jacket. If the outside world is frigid, numerous Players decide to spawn their avatars inside buildings labeled on the map as a "Gym." These spawn points give a safe place for characters to perform the jog cheat code on a moving ground machine called a treadmill.

The Earth game has an algorithm that causes stats to decrease if the character has a lack of movement around the map. Some Players complain about this algorithm and think it's a bug, but it is in fact a feature. A character decreasing in stats is one of the most powerful incentives created to keep Players active instead of setting the controller down and being unproductive. The Admin has created a string of code that boots characters for complete inactivity, and lower's the stats of characters for minimal activity. That being said, let's get into an example of how to perform this cheat code to prevent characters from becoming worse and rather boost an avatar's XP.

Imagine this scenario, the sky is paint-bucketed blue by the Design team with a hint of marine layer fog generating a crisp environment not shivering or beaming. These moments usually allow for characters to wear shorts with an athletic long sleeve. Now that the character is clothed and outside, the Player can decide to aim for achieving one of three badges: Bronze - 5-minute jog, Gold - 20-minute jog, and Diamond 40-minute jog. Today the character is planning to achieve the bronze badge. The character is outside on the street and begins stretching the legs as so:

- Reaches for the toes for a few breaths
- Pulls one knee at a time to the chest for a few breaths
- Grabs one foot at a time to the butt for a few breaths
- Wiggle the whole body at once to get the character ready

*Quick Tip: Place headphones in the character's ears to distract the avatar and make time have the illusion of going by quickly

Set a timer for five minutes. Now the character begins jogging by putting one foot in front of the other at a slow pace. The character focuses on breathing. Five minutes later, the jog is done and the character has received a stat boost on stamina and health with a trickle effect to help numerous other stats.

When doing this cheat code don't worry about the speed of the jog and rather the time of the jog. Try doing this cheat code for the avatar at least once a week and if the character starts finding jogging easy, try doing the gold badge or more and increase the frequency from once a week to a few times a week. Good luck with the cheat code and shout out to the Admin for putting this cheat code in an unlocked file so I can share the word with the rest of the Players.

CHEAT CODE #14: THANK YOU

Thank you for loading up another day in the Earth game. Thank you for a safe headquarters to recover in. Thank you for the different outfits. Thank you for the food to boost my health points. Thank you for missions. Thank you for my teammates. There is so much to be thankful for in the game, yet numerous characters will have low stats in the gratitude category. Instead of a strong gratitude skill, most characters are stuck complaining. Complaining leads to an overarching reduction across numerous stat categories. Thus, this cheat code will dull the effects of complaining by fighting complaints with gratitude. For every complaint, saying three gratuities to be thankful for are needed, according to the source code.

Inputting three things to be thankful for will slowly cause a shift in the avatar's mindset, which will lead to better results on missions. Reduction in complaints will build a stronger team. Instead of discussing missions or plans on conquering different levels in a negative light, the team will feed off of each others' optimism.

The first phase of this cheat code explains to start with gratitude for simple aspects of the game. Then over time, the avatar will create a habit of being thankful, leading to being thankful for all areas of the game. A character exerting gratitude for the little things in the game allows the character to focus more on what can be controlled in the game. By narrowing focus on the moment, the character can divert attention from the omnipotent future and remain alert for the current mission. This cheat code requires more consistency, yet only takes a few seconds to complete.

Every time you log into the game of Earth, have your character say three things they are thankful for. For example:

1. I'm thankful for my room.

2. I'm thankful for a hot shower.

3. I'm thankful for my food.

Exclaiming three things to be thankful for every morning results in stats being slightly boosted throughout the game. Doing so enhances the user experience and results in missions ending with more success than failure.

CHEAT CODE #15: LEAVE EARLY, NOT LATE

Has your character ever gone on a mission, and enjoyed the mission so much that you decided to let the character stay extra long? Then the exciting mission went from fun to horrible? Thus ruining the mission and memory? Staying too long is a universal mistake. Throughout the game, characters ruin more missions this way than actually making a poor strategic decision. Vast amounts of Players will go on interesting missions, for instance, going to the beach. The character will enjoy this new experience so much that the Player will assume the character's happiness levels and XP points will constantly increase by continuing the mission. On the contrary, 30 minutes to one hour after the peak of performance and joy, characters begin losing XP and happiness points quickly. So, what's the cheat code and solution to this common issue? Leave early.

Leaving early not only will prevent XP points and happiness levels from dwindling, yet the Admin has placed a secret 5+ XP boost if the character leaves early without complaining. Successful graphic designers in the Earth game know when to stop adding new items to their artwork because adding too many additional graphics to their design will cause the project to become overwhelming, creating a reduction in quality. Similar to sticking with missions too long. Know when to fold them. Once your character has enjoyed their time to its fullest, they make a unique cue that they are contemplating leaving. The stats show when the "stay too long" code will soon become activated. Notice this and abort the mission. Go back to the avatar's headquarters to recover and fight another day. Doing this will not only preserve energy for the next mission, yet allow that mission's XP points to be collected to the maximum. Let's go through an example.

Imagine a character is on a socialize mission that consists of attending a party with other members of the avatar's team. The mission timeline is 8 pm to midnight. Four-hour missions are exhausting towards the last hour to an hour and a half. Knowing this, the character shows up on time at 8 pm, mingles with team members, and starts saying farewell around 10:30 pm to leave at 11 pm. This will maximize the XP points and happiness levels. The character heads back to the headquarters to log out, then notices the happiness level and XP points boost.

By leaving early, the character will also be excited to do the socialize mission again. Staying too long and then leaving late creates a reluctance in the character's stats towards socialization missions. This is true amongst all missions. Don't forget, when you notice a sharp reduction in your character's enjoyment levels during a mission, leave right away to secure the XP points and happiness levels already accumulated!

CHAPTER 4

CHEAT CODE #16: WANT THE WORST, GET THE BEST

Numerous lines of code in the Earth game are purposely developed for Players to scratch their heads. No, not literally scratch their head, yet go against common understanding. Some say these ones and zeros were sequenced to help struggling characters. Similar to a safety net for trapezists. If they fall from the swings, they might feel embarrassed, but there will be no physical pain. If anything they are awarded with the freedom to fail, allowing them to practice bigger and better flips. Thus, leading to bigger and better crowds. Magically, these benefits from accepting bad situations, without complaining, lead to amazing outcomes. This cheat code explains the importance of accepting the worst during missions. Not just accepting, but choosing the worst in a situation, that way other members of the game will have the ability to receive the better options without worrying about arguing with another Player.

Have you ever been on a mission to play an activity like volleyball? The plan is to play 4 vs 4, but you are one of nine Players who are eager to play. Although your first instinct will be to feel anxiety if you will be one of the eight Players chosen to play during the first game, this is a prime opportunity for your character to gain numerous XP points. As soon as you notice this is an issue and your character displays a sense of worry, promptly exclaim "I'll wait until the next game!" Remember all the other Players are feeling the same nerves about who will not be playing. Your character doing this will lighten the mood of the whole group and instantly boost XP points by +15! This cheat code generates a powerful achievement and humility badge. Even though a character explains their willingness to sit out the first game, often that character will still play during the first game because another Player will decide to emphatically take your spot for sitting out.

Choosing the least desirable position in any situation will award characters massive XP points and possible bonus items. Bonuses are awarded when accepting the lower end of a situation in a group or one on one moments. Imagine a situation where your character's hydration meter is running low on a mission with another team member. Your character has a few sips of water in their inventory. Instead of selfishly drinking the rest, selflessly, ask the other Player in your party if they would like some water. Then have the remaining fluids second. The generous character may not benefit from a significant hydration boost at the moment, but that avatar will receive XP points. Without a doubt the moment your character is thirsty and lacking water, another character will offer your character an important hydrating potion.

Another example that is often told in ancient stories explains the importance of accepting the worst seat at a team meeting. If a character walks in and sees a seat open at a table with highly ranked avatars, which everyone is fighting for, choose to sit at the table in the back with the lower-level characters. Even if your avatar is ranked high, do this. Rather than fighting for the best seat, often the highly ranked characters will notice the cheat code of humility and invite your avatar to the prominent seat.

Want the worst and often those characters choosing this path will receive the best or close to the best. Worst case scenario, the humble character's XP will boost significantly. Making new online friends will become easier and higher-ranked members will respect the humble avatar. Effectively executing this cheat code will make life in the Earth video game easier and more enjoyable.

CHEAT CODE #17: PUZZLE PIECES

Let other Players' imaginations run wild. Friends, favorites, team members, enemies, CPUs, and all other characters in the game are gaining information about your character to solve a puzzle. Whether they know it or not, every action or word absorbed by a character is converted to a puzzle piece that continues to paint a more coherent picture of that character. Each piece gives someone more power over that Player. Knowledge is power and in interpersonal relationships this is very much so the case.

Each piece of information capable of being collected from another character makes us one step closer to understanding key factors that lead to better decisions including: trustworthiness, capabilities, usability, extortion, friendship, responsibility, avoidance, learning, and all other abilities that will translate to helping our own character level up. Giving of our own character's personal information or "Puzzle Pieces" can be used strategically or harmfully.

With every word, action, or thought of our character that enters another avatar's mind creates an ever-developing reputation. Now knowing this as a cheat code that was intentionally included in the code of the game, we can actively consider what we want other characters to know or not. To use this cheat code strategically, begin by being aware of what your character says or is associated with. According to the hard-coded cheat code documents I found in a filing cabinet, the simplest way to activate this strategy is to talk about personal topics less and reduce the amount of social media activity. Personal topics include: financial situation, relationships, opinions on controversial topics, and any other area of the Earth game you feel is sensitive.

Instead of spilling the beans on everything going on in your character's life, start filtering the content. Think before your character starts blurting out and giving out puzzle pieces unconsciously. Replace releasing these revealing thoughts with words that you want people to know about. Slow down the number of puzzle pieces being released by your character that other characters can use against your character. For example, if someone asks about how many tokens your avatar has in their account, tell them that's personal information and move on to the next conversation topic. This is one way your avatar can prevent giving away crucial puzzle pieces. On the other hand, you can have your character give away specific puzzle pieces on purpose. For example, if a character asks about an accomplishment or mission your avatar completed, give them details about that moment to allow your character's accomplishments to have some light shined on them.

Puzzle pieces can be both helpful and harmful for a character. It's impossible to filter out every word that comes out of our character's mouth to only give out strategic puzzle pieces. At the very basics of this cheat code, the Admin rewards those characters who begin thinking before they speak by deciding if their words will benefit their character or lead them to reveal too much causing XP reduction down the road.

As all Players understand, logging in begins in the character's bed. As few characters understand, the importance of achieving small wins to prepare for monumental achievements. The source code specifically has the slow drop of water in the bucket algorithm. According to the Admin, the characters that produce small wins, hence a drop of water, will receive important badges quicker than the Players that only aim for the hail mary.

The cheat code "Make the Bed" will start with the importance of starting the beginning of the day with an instant win. All a Player has to do is have their character make the bed that the avatar just woke up in since every morning it will be messy. Only one experience point will be given to the character's overall score, yet compared to the number of experience points given to other missions, "Making the Bed" is overpowered with XP. With a few seconds of time, the character receives one point, but after logging in 365 times will be, you guessed it, 365 points! Most common missions only award a character with ten XP, although taking an hour or so to complete.

Let's walk through a quick explanation of how to collect these low-hanging points. Your character spawns on the bed every morning. The "Making the Bed" XP is available as soon as your character stands up out of bed. After testing this cheat code with awareness a couple of times, I discovered that the points are only available if the bed begins being made after the first twenty minutes of getting out of bed. The trick is to place all the pillows at the head of the bed with nice organization, then tuck all the blankets in to appear flat across the layout of the bed. If the blankets are comfy-looking ones, another option is to fold them and place them towards the foot of the bed. Once complete, your character will be awarded one point! It might not sound like much, but remember that a drop in a bucket daily turns into a pale of water, and a pale of water poured into a big hole turns into a pool!

Making the character's bed as soon as the Player logs in creates a habit for the individual character to learn the importance of collecting small achievements throughout the game aside from making the bed. These other small achievements include showering in the morning, sweeping the floor, combing hair, picking up trash, and so on. Now, the next time you log into the game, make that bed!

CHEAT CODE #19: MERMAID

Just keep swimming, just keep swimming. The avatar that Players choose in the game tends to be fragile, especially the longer they play the game. Having characters train with heavy weights is fun since the results are a powerful physique that intimidates other characters during battle, yet big muscles tend to be underpowered. Rarely does the brute strength stats provide benefit during the majority of missions that are available in the game. What appears to be the most overpowered stat for missions is endurance. This endurance trickles over to other stats as well with +1, +3, and so on depending on the skill category. Rarely do Players realize the correlation between physical stats and mental stats. Training the character to physically push themselves will allow the avatar to become relentless during missions that require both mental and physical skills to earn more badges.

The Developers included water all over the map for numerous reasons. One of those reasons being for Players to take their character's to the water to learn how to swim. Even more importantly, learning to swim long distances. There are numerous tutorial videos that characters have compiled on in-game apps to help other avatars learn to swim. Although there are plenty of skills for a character to learn on these app platforms, including running, biking, and other activities, swimming remains superior. The learning curve for swimming can be daunting if the character's swimming stats are innately low. Don't be discouraged if this is the case, rather, be motivated! The more difficult a skill is initially for a character, the more points they are rewarded. You might be wondering: "Well where can I swim and what do I need?" Great questions, here are some answers.

Players can take their character swimming with as little as some swimming shorts and nothing more. One item that can be acquired for a few coins, and will make a huge impact on swimming success are "goggles." These can be found at numerous stores on the map or purchased on the Players' hub to be delivered to their headquarters. Let's walk through an example:

Bring your character to a local gym on the map that has an indoor pool. Indoor pools are great for characters just learning to swim. In the future, try taking your avatar to open water, for instance, an ocean or lake. Once your character arrives at the pool, grab a towel and the goggles item. Take these to the pool. Choose an empty lane. Open your hub, and type in "how to swim freestyle." Watch the video to learn the controls of swimming, then try to see if your character is a natural or not. Have your character focus and try swimming for only 10 minutes, not more or less. Then dry off and head back to the headquarters. Try to go swimming once a week until the Player is comfortable in the water. Most likely, your character will struggle with swimming properly when trying proper technique for the first time. Water will often go in their nose for the first couple of swimming sessions. The cheat code explains to only do 10 minute sessions to avoid a character from losing interest in swimming due to the initial steep learning curve. Once they are able to do this cheat code for six to eight sessions, the activity will feel more natural thus giving the character a massive XP boost.

This cheat code might require more effort to see a skill improvement but is worth a rare badge. Not many Players have taken the time to train their character to learn the proper way to swim. Especially long distances. When you are ready to push your character to the next level with this powerful cheat code, grab a towel and goggles then make your way to a pool!

CHEAT CODE #20: USE THE MED-KIT

The Creators of the game have cursed the aloof Players. The Earth game does this in the form of weeding out the weak and allowing the strong to survive. Frequently on the leaderboards Players will see those characters that were doing so well, yet drastically lose the game, nearly spontaneously. This miraculous death or massive XP reduction stems from a lack of taking the character's health bar seriously. Unlike other video games that allow the health to remain stagnant until impacted by an outside force, or in some games will increase over time, the Earth game's health bar drops like a rock in water if overlooked.

Minor flesh wounds or slight bruising, tend to recover back to full strength without needing to use a med kit, although, the majority of health bar reducers need to be met with an instant med kit cheat code. If a Player decides that the character will be fine without further examination after taking a critical hit during a mission, that wound will prevent future missions. Seeking immediate medical attention from a local health location in the form of a hospital or medical store will allow characters to heal then giving them the option to join missions again soon. Deciding to act as if the wound does not exist can cause the character to be inactive on the account for weeks. Also, the Admin updated the game so that if a Player decides to neglect the character's health, a randomized code fires between 1-1000, which if the number lands correctly will cause the character to be booted from the game. The proactive and immediate are rewarded in the Earth game, unlike the lazy and sloth. Let's go through an example.

A Player decides to take his avatar on a surfing mission. The character named Waylan is enjoying catching numerous waves until wiping out with damage dealt to the ear. After Waylan hits his head on the board, water is injected into the ear, causing the avatar's ear canal to grow damp with perfect conditions for bacteria to multiply. Waylan could decide to wait weeks hoping for the ear to heal and reinstate the hearing, yet remembers another character doing the surfing mission attempted this strategy, causing permanent hearing loss. Remembering the cheat code "Use the Med-Kit" Waylan decides to find the nearby hospital on the map and receive concise medicine. The medicine stopped the infection and allowed the character to keep the ear hearing. Waylen was able to go back to the surfing mission after a few days with full health, instead of quickly declining his ear health with the potential of death.

Next time your character experiences health damage, seek immediate medical attention. Do not wait. Quickly treating the issue will allow the avatar to heal. Waiting often causes the health to spiral out of control to the point of no return. In the Earth game, there's no time travel…yet. Possibly on a future update, but no one is anticipating time travel to be inputted into the game in the short future. So until then, all characters are stuck with needing to make health decisions at the moment they occur. This is true for all health events:

sicknesses, abrasions, impact, broken bones, torn muscles, and all other health-reducing events. The healthier the character, the more enjoyable the game.

CHAPTER 5

CHEAT CODE #21: ADDING FRIENDS

Big stat boosts for making friends! Spending time alone provides XP to an extent. Too much time alone will end up causing a deterioration in the mental health chart. Avatars typically come pre-equipped with two styles of personalities that can help or hinder friendship development. The Dev team decided to name these two traits: extrovert and introvert. Extroverts are naturally boosted with social skills since the character came preinstalled with this enhancement. Introverts, on the other hand, feel most comfortable hanging out with themselves. Both of these styles are capable of making deep friendships. Whichever label your avatar falls into, ignore thinking that one is better than the other for adding meaningful friendships.

This adding friends cheat code explains the importance of taking initiative as opposed to waiting for friendship to appear from thin air. Depending on the avatar's stats, talking with other Players can cause butterflies of anxiety. The XP boost for going out of the way to make a new friend is 3x greater than the satisfaction of being aloof. Remaining unwilling to interact with other Players gives a quick happiness boost to Players' characters, but then follows with pain that reduces the mental health stat.

Is there another avatar you enjoyed spending time with, but have yet to add them as a friend by receiving their contact code? Turning that character from an acquaintance to a friend will increase XP by 40 simply by getting their contact code. The few awkward seconds it takes to ask the other Player, "Can I get your number and I'll let you know next time I go on this mission," is so quick that both characters forget the potential odd feeling. Next time there is another character you'd like to learn more about, count down: 3, 2, 1, and force your avatar to ask for their number. The next 40 XP boost comes from being brave enough to text them to join a mission. BEWARE: Do not text them too frequently or soon. This will cause an XP reduction because your character is displaying desperation. Wait to text them at the right moment. Don't force the interaction. Next time you notice a mission that you both are comfortable with, casually text them. If they say no, in any fashion, it's okay! Friends are simply another instrument in your band. Songs can be beautiful with one instrument. Songs can also sound pleasant with 2, 3, 4, or more instruments. None innately better or worse.

Friendship is NOT your new drug. Making friends requires wanting the other person to be happy and enjoy time together, yet not becoming dependent on the new friend. Ask your character often: "Would I be happy without this person?" If yes, great! If no, slowly reframe your avatar's thinking to wanting them to be happy instead of them making you happy. Also, if this happens where the majority of your friendship XP is flowing from one character, it's time to diversify! Start with the main portion of this cheat code explaining how to find more friends. Having a few friends to boost XP with, is better than having one because if they leave the team, your character will be critically hit to the mental health stat.

On the other hand, possibly the other character has developed a need for an overwhelming amount of attention to make them feel better, but this is draining your character's energy. In this circumstance, tell this mantra to your avatar: "I'd rather be happy than have you." Letting go of friends, creating boundaries, and freeing up energy for your character is okay. Some of the most painful moments in the Earth game are caused by other characters draining the mental health stat. Comprehending this pain is more difficult than physical pain because it is invisible. Would you allow your character to hold a flaming hot ball? No, you would let it go. Same thing with friendships, if you can identify the exact source of pain from a friend, it's time to drop the flaming hot friend. Once let go, give yourself some distance from the friend and possibly they will cool down and be capable of being held again.

When there's a character that you would like to learn more about, go get their number! Wait for the right moment, text them, and enjoy a mission to get the friendship off the ground. Who knows, it can result in reciprocal XP boosts for the rest of both of your Earth seasons.

CHEAT CODE #22: BE THE CHANGE

What's easier, changing every Player in the game or changing yourself to make a higher quality overall community in the Earth game? Be the change you want to see in the game. If a Player notices a group of characters being rude, talking with them about their issue might just enhance their negativity. Instead, the Admin coded the game in a way that forces characters to be more self-introspective to make a difference. Avatar's emotions are coded as contagious. If one character is sad, characters within 0-15 feet will experience an increase in their avatar's sadness levels. Vise versa, if a character is outwardly happy, other avatars nearby will receive a boost in their happiness.

Rather than worrying about others changing their ways, focus on having your character be the living body of the change you seek. If a Player wants to see more compliments occurring in the game as opposed to criticism, then that Player needs to have their character begin complimenting others. Since all emotional activity was developed to be contagious, it's imperative to have the character represent, in this circumstance, complementary actions. Let's go through the direct path on how to perform the "Be the Change" cheat code.

Pretend there is a character named Bob who has a roommate named Charlie. Bob wants the house to be cleaner and believes Charlie is the reason for the house being dirty. Bob learns about the "Be the Change" issue, then decides that the best way for Charlie to begin cleaning more is for Bob himself to clean more often. Bob starts cleaning the house during times when Charlie can notice. The cheat code's contagious effect stimulates Charlie's stats, causing Charlie to clean more frequently. Instead of Bob complaining or continually bickering Charlie, he was the change he wanted to see in the world, thus stimulating those around him to become more cleanly as well.

Once a Player decides the change they want to see in the world, then the next step is simply to take action. No more sitting around waiting for the world to change. Begin the change right now and watch how the snowball effect will cause those around your character to change for the better.

As soon as you log in, have your character brush their teeth. Right before logging out, have your character brush and floss their teeth. Teeth are the most recognized part of a character's body that is noticed for any flaws. A piece of food in their teeth is nearly impossible for another character to unnotice. Unhealthy teeth that are yellow or blackening not only cause other characters to realize the flaw but lower your character's confidence bar. Aside from the confidence stat, unhealthy teeth, and gums can cause a level 10 out of 10 damage to a character. This amount of damage being caused in the same vicinity as the avatar's brain will lower their thinking stamina, which severely damages their ability to complete missions to their fullest potential.

As simple as brushing in the morning and then brushing and flossing at night remains difficult for the majority of the game's population. One minute in the morning and two minutes at night of dental hygiene is the most overpowered XP boost in the whole game. According to the Dev team, this XP boost was not done purposely, yet having consistently clean teeth became a major part of the game organically. Having healthy teeth helps a Player's character in numerous facets of the game for example: health, confidence, social skills, and eating. Poor care of teeth results in the inability to eat food comfortably which leads to a spiral of other issues. If one side of a character's teeth can only be used, then those teeth will become overused causing quicker decay thus leading to both sides of the mouth being damaged. Once a character finally realizes something needs to be done to prevent this backward trend, the number of tokens required to fix these tooth issues can cause a character to completely exhaust their savings.

All these issues and setbacks stem from neglecting these two simple tasks of brushing and flossing. To properly perform this cheat code, a Player needs to, at a minimum, brush their teeth after logging in, then brush and floss their teeth before logging out without eating or drinking anything afterward that is not water. Once you decide to login to the game of Earth, have your character find their toothbrush and toothpaste then proceed to brush their teeth for 45-60 seconds. Once you are done playing with the character for the day and know they are done eating and drinking everything aside from water, then have your character brush their teeth for the 45-60 seconds again. After brushing the teeth, have the character floss their teeth. The simplest way to stay consistent with flossing is to purchase a bag of "floss picks" and put the bag directly next to the character's bed. Once they lay down in the bed the character can casually reach over to the bag of floss and gently floss between each tooth. Be sure to lightly floss the very back teeth as well. When flossing, use a see-saw motion of gently going up and down with the floss string/pick. Stray from rubbing the string aggressively on the gums and assuming the harder the character flosses the cleaner. Instead, this will aggravate the character's gums. Feel free to do some research for the proper technique on flossing. Once flossing is complete, throw the floss on the floor, then the next time you log in, have the character throw away yesterday's floss.

This simple cheat code will boost your character's overall abilities and XP more than any other 2-3 minute mission in the whole game. Taking the time to be consistent with brushing and flossing will allow the character to feel healthier, look better, think more clearly, and continue to level up. Next time your character is shopping at the store, have them spend their tokens to better themselves by purchasing floss, a toothbrush, and toothpaste.

Have you ever taken your character on a long run? Did you have your avatar sprint their fastest or did they set a manageable pace? In order to finish long runs, the characters need to run at a sustainable pace or else the energy bar depletes rapidly thus causing them to black out which results in severe damage taken to the overall stats. This damage is not restricted to only occurring during a character's physical activity. So what else can create a similar degree of energy reduction? Saying yes too often. Accepting overwhelming amounts of missions for a character to quest on will trigger the overwhelming code to activate resulting in the energy bar to free fall and rejuvenate slower than physical activity energy loss. Saying yes to missions is critical for the growth of a character to level up properly, yet Players need to be conscious of their energy bar or the character will level down. Contrary to popular belief, refusing to do missions will not only boost energy but earn badges for the character and XP points for leveling up.

This cheat code, nonetheless, is called "No." If the character's energy bar is half of its potential energy, decline the next mission. Wait for the energy bar to climb past the halfway point. As long as the avatar's energy is above 50% the character will not lose XP points. A character's stamina varies throughout the game. A variety of character types will be capable of accepting numerous missions daily prior to dropping below the 50% energy point. Other character types will have a deficiency in the energy stamina stat causing even one mission daily to significantly reduce energy below 50%. The common rule of thumb is to say "No" to all missions except one per day. A Player will be able to feel out their character's energy capabilities and pivot to increase or reduce mission acceptance. Let's walk through an example:

Below is a list of missions that appeared in one character's dashboard during a day and the proper way to accept or decline:

1. Join other team members for a surf day (NO)

2. Learn how to play the guitar (YES)

3. Attend a full moon dance party (NO)

These are three missions that came on the dashboard for a character whose energy bar was 75%. Missions involving interactions with team members or random Players typically cost 30%+ of energy. Thus, causing this character to accept a mission with minimal hit points to the energy bar. Keep a close eye on your character's energy bar and do NOT be reluctant to say the magical and XP-inducing word "No."

CHEAT CODE #25: SNOWBALL EFFECT

All characters have a mission list, idea board, and inventory that continues to update throughout the game. The mission list is a perpetual to-do list that can either be added by an individual Player or by other Players adding missions to your character's board to earn XP points. A mission can be different ways to earn more tokens in the game, which usually looks like laborious activities. For example, driving inventory to other characters' headquarters. Or these missions can be self-elected. For example, having the character learn a new skill or visit a new location. Learning guitar or exploring the beach. An idea board is sprung about from the character's mind. These are generated seemingly out of nowhere, yet the ideas come from a simple "if-then" statement found in the code. The idea boards constantly generate. Although, the rate at which ideas formulate depends on the avatar's activity. If the character is consuming information on minimalist missions, then the idea board will slowly accumulate. Doing constant missions, especially difficult or missions that involve a completely new style of thinking will add more ideas rapidly. Inventory is physical items that can be received by the character through missions or purchases. This cheat code will focus on the idea board.

Characters focusing on developing a dynamic and lengthy idea board level up quicker than having numerous items or mission completeness by themselves. Thus, this cheat code will revolve around how to acquire the most ideas that appear on the board. All characters are aware of the formation of ideas and most Players decide that these ideas are distractions or are unimportant. Little do the majority of characters know the XP bonuses received by those avatars that decide to write down the fleeting idea. Ideas will come and go on the board. Usually, ideas will be written in the mind of the avatar for a few minutes to a day, eventually fading away until the character will not be able to remember the novel idea. For example, a character might be on a mission and think of a life-changing idea like "I would like to write a book on cheat codes for the Earth game." Rather than daydreaming about this thought until it disappears forever, have your character open up the notes app on their electronic device to write down the idea. This way, even though your character might not be ready to do the idea that instant, the avatar can come back to the thought, later on, to decide whether to act on the idea or not. At least the idea will get an infinite life span now that it is written down.

Finding these ideas is similar to finding easter eggs in different games. The Player needs to take their character on missions and immerse the avatar in unique scenarios. Accept invitations to uncompleted missions. If your character has yet to experience swimming in the ocean, go for a swim in the ocean. If your character has not read many books, find audiobooks or physical books and begin having the avatar download information. Maybe the character has yet to make a deep friendship with another avatar, then next time the opportunity comes about, be open to vulnerability and enjoy the character's thoughts and presence. Choosing to complete these missions allows the idea board to generate vast amounts of ideas. Similar to fishing, the more missions a character does is equivalent to having numerous fishing lines in the water. With more lines gives the character's mind a better chance of generating useful ideas.

Once these thoughts begin generating more often, remember to have the avatar write down the idea as quickly as possible. Although it might feel simple, each time the character writes down a new idea, doing so instantly allows the avatar's XP to increase which boosts the characters level instantly. Continue to write down all the character's ideas, and you will be amazed by how these ideas help lead the avatar's journey in a beautiful new direction full of leveling up. Don't force ideas, they will come simply by having the character exposed to new missions.

CHEAT CODE #26: AGREE WITH THEM

Has your character ever been insulted by another character? Here is a cheat code that can reduce the damage taken to your character's shields. Although this input still causes some reduction to your avatar's health, it is more so to prevent a flurry of attacks that lead to critical hit points.

Once your character starts experiencing that tingly feeling in the chest that the Admin developed as a pop-up for conflict, try your best to remember this step-by-step code. Use your character's mouth and vocal cords to conjure up the phrase "Yeah you're probably right." To enhance the effects of this cheat code, have your character's facial expressions do a slight smile during this cheat code input. This will create the illusion of being genuine before you become truly genuine at this code. Let's walk through a scenario where your Player might encounter this kind of interaction with one of the other characters.

Let's say your character's username is "Steve" and the insulter's character's name is "Billy."

Steve: *Joins a pickup basketball game on the Chicago map*

Billy: *Currently on the winning team with his friends then begins playing against Steve's team*

Steve: *Misses a layup*

Billy: "Dude you're really bad at basketball, why are you even playing?"

Steve: *Remembering the cheat code just before taking too many hit points* "Yeah you're probably right."

Billy: *Startled and proceeds to play it off like he was kidding, then gives a pointer on how to make a layup easier to Steve* "I'm just messing with you. I was bad at first too. I found out that aiming higher off the backboard helps layups go in more often. Give it a try next time."

Steve: *Realizing the cheat code was inputted correctly* "Thanks, I love watching basketball, but haven't played very much. I'll try your advice next time!"

This "Agree with Them" cheat code has a different range of effects based on your character's input ability and the insulter's skill level. In the worst-case scenario, the insulting character won't feel as much of a need to insult again. Also, if other characters are nearby, they typically send out a disapproval attack, causing a high level of damage to the insulting character. The disapproval attack can cause the insulter to lose social achievements from their inventory. These social achievements will be even more difficult to recover after a disapproval attack.

Your character, if the cheat code is done correctly, can receive the "Self Confidence" social achievement. This achievement will go into your inventory as a bronze award. It is not permanent, yet it can level up to gold then diamond. Fall back on this achievement during times when your Player experiences the "doubt" roadblock. Remember the time you received this "Self Confidence" achievement to give your character a boost of confidence during inevitable doubtful missions.

Beautifully, this specific cheat code can also be customized if your character has creativity as a strength. The foundation of this cheat code is to agree with the insulting character. Whether you want to say "Yeah, you're right." or even do an advanced "Agree with Them" cheat code by being sarcastic. For instance in the previous example: "Man I am bad at layups and basketball. My goal is to miss 10 layups today." Hopefully, this cheat code benefits your character and helps it level up throughout the game. Good luck!

CHAPTER 6

CHEAT CODE #27: CONSISTENT BEDTIME

Go to sleeeeep, go to sleeeeep little character. Have you ever been using your character in first person and the view appears fuzzy with long blinks? Your avatar is sleepy! I know, it's a strange concept. From what we understand, the Dev team was unsure of including this feature, because including required sleeping which would vastly decrease active users and total playtime. What we do know, characters need to close those video injectors for roughly 8 hours daily. These video injectors are called "eyes" and are located typically on the front of an avatar's body.

This feature, which is a feature and not a bug, remains odd, due to all the characters in the game needing to take a break for 8 hours which reduces productivity by 33%. The research team for this cheat code concluded that sleeping for 8 hours is a constant responsibility test. Most importantly, having your character fall asleep and wake up at a consistent time is paramount. Thus, this cheat code for Players to understand and implement can be an overpowered input if done correctly. Let's walk through an example.

To begin, you would need to guide your avatar to a safe and quiet area away from other characters and NPCs. You are at your most vulnerable in this 8-hour detour, so be sure to lock doors and cuddle up in a building that preferably has your team to watch the doors if danger emerges. Remember that tip about going to bed and waking up at the same time, let's talk about it. What time do you need to be awake to achieve time-sensitive tasks like work and school? Let's say you want to work on collecting badges every day at 9 am. If that is the case, characters are slow when waking up so this cheat code explains the importance of waking up two hours before starting a mission. That being said, your avatar will wake up at 7 am daily. Now backtrack to the magic eight number. That puts the sleep time at 11 pm. If you want to copy this cheat code down to the moment, lay your character down and close the eyes at 11 pm then wake up at 7 am. Numerous characters prefer using their phone to set an alarm for 7 am daily.

Easy enough, right? Welp, this is one of the most widely known cheat codes in the game, yet few chose to take advantage. Let's see if you as a Player can utilize this cheat code to give your character the massively overpowered energy boost. Sleeping for eight hours and doing so at a consistent time increases stats that include: energy, focus, creativity, alertness, sociability, and much more! Also, this cheat code has an easter egg inside, called "dreaming." It's like a free brand-new episode of the most random stuff, with your character as the star in the cast. Sweet dreams!

CHEAT CODE #28: SPEAK KINDLY

Never say anything bad about anyone and your character will prosper on the Team. Speaking kindly about everyone is an ancient cheat code that has worked for relationship building since season one. Gossiping or complaining about other characters might feel good at the moment, yet the Developers set up this update called the Karma effect. If a Player's avatar speaks negatively about others, the negative-speaking character will receive negativity in return. Although that might seem harsh, this leads us to one of the most wondrous cheat codes: using the karma effect to create positive outcomes. Speaking positively about other avatars, especially when those characters are not nearby, leads to positive results. These positive results will fall into the gameplay in a few different ways. Successful missions start happening more frequently, more team members want to help your character prosper, and most importantly, the positive speaking avatar will have significant boosts on their social stats.

An increase in social stats is a river stat. Meaning having this character quality strong, will trickle to side stream abilities including confidence, happiness, less depression and anxiety, and much more. Only speaking positively and seeing the best in other characters reduces the amount of criticism that comes back to your character. Interestingly, all characters in the Earth game will inherently have one positive quality. This is in the code. Every time your character thinks to critique another avatar, pause and concentrate to determine that avatar's quality. When conversing with a team member about another character, downplay the negative aspect of the avatar, then replace your character's words with a compliment. The majority of gossip makes its way back to the character being talked about. Saying another character is a loose screw might as well be direct messaged to that character. Over time, one character will tell a friend that tells a friend that tells the recipient. If your character speaks poorly, then your character will end up losing social points. On the contrary, if your character speaks compliments, that compliment will make its way eventually to the spoken upon character. Thus, creating a boost in social points.

For instance, there is an avatar named Lamp who is speaking with a team member named Kees. They are discussing another team member's performance in a recent mission, named Rubi. Rubi struggled with endurance during this previous performance. Lamp thinks to complain about Rubi's lack of endurance. Considering it to be an absence of commitment to the mission. Luckily Lamp remembers the "Speak Kindly" cheat code, pauses the critical thought, then replaces the idea with, "Rubi did well the week before, although her endurance was slightly lower, her ability to recoup and come back stronger is contagious. I can't wait to join the mission with her again." Kees, thinking a negative remark would come from Lamp, is stunned and feels more inclined to speak compliments as well. Kees sees Rubi a few logins later and says "Lamp thinks highly of your abilities and feels that your endurance was low last mission, but you have a strong avatar that will bounce back and impress. Keep up the great work!"

Imagine that every word that comes out of your character's mouth will end up being regurgitated to that avatar you were discussing. Speak poorly and that character will end up biting your avatar back in some way down the road. Speak complimentically and your character will receive positive XP points from that Player in return.

CHEAT CODE #29: CONSCIOUSLY SPEAK

The majority of the time characters are acting and speaking mindlessly. Using premade responses or unthoughtful remarks. Conversing in this manner typically results in no major effects, yet a regretful statement might slip out. Thus causing a character's social stats to take a critical hit.

This cheat code is more difficult to incorporate due to Players constantly keeping their characters busy with tasks and missions. Constant missions and tasks mean the avatar is typically on a thinking train that is difficult to stop. Next time your character is about to talk with another character, input into their mind: "Think Before Speaking." Once you are successful with reminding your character of this simple phrase before a few conversations, remembering before future interactions will become easier. By thinking before speaking, your character will begin speaking consciously instead of from the subconscious. Once an avatar begins talking with others thoughtfully, then your character will become less regretful with what they say to others. Slowly, every thought-out sentence gives your character's social stats a boost of +1 XP per sentence.

Let's walk through an example. Imagine a character named Moon is approached by a depressive character named Star. Star begins venting to Moon about their past difficulties. Typically Moon would respond unthoughtfully and sometimes cause Star more pain than relief. This time, Moon decided to use the "Consciously Speak" cheat code. He inputted the code through the keyboard into his character's mind, "Think Before Speaking." Doing this, made Moon take one extra second to think about their response to Star. Resulting in a well-thought-out sentence giving Star a sense of relief from their depressive feelings. Moon gave Star five thoughtful sentences resulting in an accumulation of +5 XP.

A seemingly small cheat code like "Consciously Speaking" racks up numerous points throughout a game session. Speaking is done constantly with other avatars and becoming more aware of the words flowing out of a character's mind will not only help the social stats, but will also make missions easier to complete due to better communication. During your character's next conversation with another avatar, input the thought "Think Before Speaking."

CHEAT CODE #30: WHY SO SERIOUS?

It's just a game. At the end of the day, the Earth game does not actually mean much. The Dev team had an idea, spent some time on the design and functionality then put it on the market. The Admin did not think it would become this popular. They actually thought the Earth game was going downhill after a few major bugs nearly caused the servers to be unplugged. The legendary meteor bug which was not so much a bug because a former Admin, who would then be fired, sent a rogue meteor from space to hit the Earth game in hopes of taking the HP from all the characters. Luckily, the game continued! Some argue that the meteor bug took the game down a better path, with well-thought-out updates and gameplay. Any Player's character can lose all their HP at any moment causing them to be kicked from the game and resetting back to level one with a new avatar. Knowing this is liberating rather than stressful. At any moment or during any mission, even the easy ones, your character can be sent back to level one. So don't take this game too seriously, instead have fun!

Players are the ones who choose to download this Earth game. Each character did not have to be created, but since they were created, enjoy the Earth game to its fullest. No need to rage quit and leave the game early. If you lose a mission, don't take it personally, it's just a game. If a Player wants to leave your team it's okay, it's just a game. They too want to be happy with their gaming experience. Maybe your character applied to join a group to learn more about how to increase a character's monetary value and was declined. It's okay, no need to take it seriously, this is just a game. Try joining a different group or doing a different mission. This cheat code explains to not feel too exhilarated after a successful mission and not become too depressed after failure. At any moment, high or low, have your character say out loud or in their minds: "This too will pass." Let's go through some examples.

In this example we will see how one character handles success without taking it so seriously then another character will experience failure without taking it so seriously. A character named Suzy entered a mission to run twenty-six miles against a thousand other avatars. Suzy practices for months, runs the race and comes in first place. Suzy is ecstatic, yet realizes these emotions "too will pass." Thus says to herself, "This too will pass." Even though it's a positive moment, no reason to take it too seriously because in the end, this is just a game. Many characters will experience success and start feeling like they are more important than other avatars. Feeling this way will cause a decline in XP points and cause the avatar to increase their anxiety levels. This happens since that character assumes they have to remain winning, even though all characters will eventually lose during the game in some sort of fashion. Players that keep winning from a realistic perspective will not only receive the successful mission badge but increase their XP.

On the other end of the spectrum, a character can fail. During Suzy's race, there was another racer named Paul. Paul trained for weeks, yet came in eight hundred and fiftieth place. Paul thought he would at least be in the top one hundred. He told all his team members that he'll make them proud and be in the top 10%. Coming in the bottom 20% caused Paul some pain of failure. That pain too will pass. In the same way, the joy of winning will pass, and the pain of losing will pass. Paul remembers this and has his character use the cheat code by saying: "This too will pass." Paul still feels pain at the moment, yet the pain does not sink too deep and prevents the depression stat from increasing uncontrollably. Now Paul can turn this loss into a win by realizing that the energy of losing will boost his character's learning stats. Characters learn more during losses than wins, which paradoxically makes losing, winning. Putting losing into this lens boosts characters' XP points by +10.

Remember, during big moments of emotion whether positive or negative, immediately insert this cheat code. Have the character say once or numerous times, "This too will pass" during any emotional moment. The Earth game will inevitably allow each character to experience numerous wins and losses. Enjoy the emotions that come with both those experiences and good luck with your missions!

CHEAT CODE #31: FORGIVE

Forgiving in the Earth game is equivalent to locating excess data on a computer and then deleting it to free up storage. The character's mind can only handle so much data at one time to think about and focus on. Between missions, relationships, creative thinking, and other thoughts going on at all times, the avatar's mind has a finite amount of bandwidth to maintain productivity. The typical stock character's mind can focus on three different aspects of the game per day. Usually, a character will contemplate about an upcoming mission, a friend, and what they plan on eating that day. After three points of focus in one day, the mind starts to lose signal strength.

In this cheat code, we will look at one of the biggest storage cloggers across the game according to the Dev team. Since the Earth game is an open-source game, allowing the future seasons to be determined by the Players themselves, the Dev team watches the data develop organically instead of coding in every possibility. To their surprise, the thoughts that caused the most unnecessary amounts of storage to be used were characters not forgiving each other. By not forgiving another character, an avatar would continuously think about them negatively, without hoping to resolve issues.

By not forgiving and moving on, characters find themselves in a loop putting mental storage towards characters that are of no benefit to their growth. If one character physically or emotionally harms another character, the receiver of the pain will grow a distaste for the other. Even after a character decides to create boundaries with the harmful character by not talking, seeing, or interacting with them, without forgiving the harmful character will still linger in the mind. Thus, the last step to close the loop and free up storage in your avatar's mind is to forgive that character. This does not mean your character has to go to the other avatar and verbally forgive, instead, your character needs to forgive in their own mind. To perform this cheat code correctly, insert these words into your character's mind: "I forgive you (insert name here). I want you to be happy and free from suffering."

Let's walk through an example of what this may look like. A character named Thalia is friends with another character named Ann. The two of them would go on missions a few times a week together until one day Ann became an angry character and yelled at Thalia for no reason. Thalia's feelings were hurt and she decided she wouldn't hang out with Ann anymore, but still found herself thinking about the times Ann yelled at her. Thalia came across the forgiveness cheat code and inputted it into the character's mind: "I forgive you, Ann. I want you to be happy and free from suffering." Although the pain was not instantly relieved, the person was forgiven which allows the pain to begin the process of slowly drifting away.

Is there a character your avatar has interacted with who caused pain that continues to linger in their mind? Maybe there is one avatar that comes to mind or multiple. However many it may be, this cheat code can be used an unlimited amount of times and is just as effective if not more every time the cheat code is performed. Try this cheat code today and watch how the storage in your character's mind begins to free up space and boost their contentment stats instantly.

CHEAT CODE #32: COUNTING BREATHS

Your character is constantly breathing, without ever worrying that they'll stop. Crazy, I know. It's what some of the higher-level avatars call subconscious. Something happening without the character using the controller or keyboard to generate a response. What's wonderful about this subconscious feature of a character, it's a hybrid. Meaning, breathing can be conscious as well. Unbeknownst, a Player can have the character bring breathing from the subconscious to the conscious to elicit a health boost. These health boosts require no tokens or demand a special location to generate a health increase.

This cheat code needs zero prerequisites, minimal effort provides substantiate health boost, yet, rarely this cheat code is discovered by Players. It's believed that a team of avatars called, Monks, discovered the power of breathing consciously. Since the game's release, numerous Players have tried to take the breathing technique formula and convert it to different more complicated breathing techniques, which are wonderful as well, but this simple cheat code is all that is needed to provide a vast health boost.

To perform this breathing cheat code, have your character turn their attention towards their breath. The character might be breathing through the nose, mouth, or both. Possibly deep breaths or shallow breaths. Much of how the breathing is happening is unimportant. What matters is that the character notices the breath going in and then going out. Simply, the cheat code states to have the character count the inhale and exhale of their breaths all the way up to 60. The inhale counts as one and the exhale counts as one. After thirty complete breaths, the cheat code will be complete. Time for an example.

A character decides to do this breathing technique by sitting down on a chair. Although the cheat code can be completed lying down, sitting, standing, or moving. This avatar closes their eyes, although keeping them open is fine. The avatar focuses on the breath and breaths in, thus counting as one. Then exhaling, counting as two. Inhaling again, three. Exhaling, four. Inhaling, five. Exhaling, six. Up to sixty. After reaching sixty inhales plus exhales, the Admin has coded the operating system to kick out an immediate health boost to the character.

The health boosts accumulated from this "Counting Breaths" cheat code, allow characters to perform missions more acutely since they are less antsy and more settled down. Causing them to perform strategic moves and physical activity with more precision. Next time your character is experiencing low health whether on the physical or psychological bar, try this cheat code to turn the downward trend around. Even in moments of high health, try this cheat code proactively, to prevent a health reduction. Enjoy your daily missions with extra health now!

CHAPTER 7

CHEAT CODE #33: SHARE THE HEADQUARTERS

Even with so many Players logging in daily to the most popular game in the world, a character can easily increase the lonely stats. The Earth game provides avatars with a double-edged sword that is deeply coded into each avatar's stats. Being alone causes a character to boost contentment, yet too much solitude causes that content feeling to disappear and turn into an acute increase in depression. Luckily, I found a cheat code in one of the Dev's files and realized the most important input to battle against loneliness in a character.

Find a roommate to share your character's headquarters with. Maybe one, two, or even three other Players. Not just any kind of Player though. Share a log-in place with Players that you enjoy doing missions with the most. Choosing to share a place with Players that do not suit your avatar's personality could do damage to the health factor. This is one of the most difficult cheat codes to successfully incorporate. With great risk comes an insurmountable reward. Up to 50+ XP points are added to the happiness stat. Creating a safe headquarters, filled with one to three friends, allows your character's mental health shields to boost at twice the speed during recovery.

Although, sharing the space with random potentially harmful avatars slows or even reverses recovery. Having a toxic headquarters is equivalent to remaining on a harmful mission even during time away from the battlefield. Not only will the character's personal stats increase, the avatar's inventory, and tokens will increase as well.

Sharing a space with team members causes the price of the headquarters to be reduced, allocating food amongst the household reduces the price for health boost items due to buying in bulk, and being around other characters gives Players a way to discuss strategies and intel for the next mission. Uncovering new learning badges occurs quicker with having a shared headquarters by learning tendencies, knowledge, and social skills with each other.

To successfully input the "Share the Headquarters" cheat code, start by writing down a list of the usernames that you enjoy doing missions with. Put them in a list from best to worst on who your character would prefer sharing a space. Are the characters nice, productive, clean, conflictive, calm, share mission preferences, and any other characteristics important to your avatar? Once you choose one to three friends, search for a headquarters, move in, and watch your character's stats increase.

The most important part of this cheat code is being concise with choosing who to share the headquarters with. It is better to live with one perfect fit, than two mediocre friends. Pick wisely and enjoy the company and badges that come with sharing a headquarters!

CHEAT CODE #34: DON'T FORCE

Over time anything is possible to develop. Would you like your character to make a new friend, romantic relationship, business, or be invited to certain missions? Being desperate is the quickest way to divert from any of these hopes. Trying to force a situation rather than allowing the timeline to fold out naturally will cause wrinkles in plans. Similar to cooking food, thawing food from the freezer on a pan with a flame on high will only burn the outside and leave the inside frozen. Meeting a new friend and asking them to go on a mission every day will cause the relationship to be forced too quickly and the two characters could get annoyed with each other rather than slowly cooking the relationship into something beautiful and long-lasting.

If your avatar wants to join a "create your own business" mission, this requires patience as well. Forcing a business to grow instead of allowing the business to create a foundation, will cause the character to be disappointed and the business to be fragile. Instead, have the avatar think long-term. Assume the business will take 4-5 seasons to start making a noticeable impact that creates profitable tokens.

Possibly your next goal is to develop a romantic relationship. Give the relationship time to develop if your character is attracted to a particular avatar. Being overzealous or seeming desperate was coded to make the other avatar want to be distant. The characters in the game were all developed to desire less those that want them desperately. When a character is trying too hard to hang out with another character, then that other character's danger radar starts blinking. Instead of feeling attracted by someone showing excess love, characters feel as if they are in danger and avoid those that are trying to force a relationship rather than allow a natural development.

Rather than forcing a situation to happen, give it time. Look to allow the relationships or missions to grow over time. Stray from hoping for a quick turnaround in any circumstance. Anything worthwhile is not quick and anything quick is not worth anything. Next time you are hoping for a situation to unfold favorably, assume it will take more than one season and focus on the missions that you do have instant control over.

CHEAT CODE #35: DON'T SAY SORRY

Would you like your character to have low confidence? Here's an anti-cheat code. Every time your character does one little thing wrong, constantly say sorry. Show up to a mission a minute late, say sorry. Accidentally forget to bring extra water for the team, plead sorry. Another character is upset, clearly not because of your avatar, say sorry. Doing these will create a lovely decline in any character's confidence levels.

Now that the sarcasm is out of the way, let's discuss how to have a character's confidence increase rather than decline. Stay away from the "S" word, "sorry." Unless "sorry" is being used to show your genuine condolences, do NOT say sorry! Every time a character exclaims the "S" word, their confidence stat loses 1 point. Okay, losing one point might feel insignificant, oh the contrary. One drop of water every hour on an unthatched roof will cause the dwelling to collapse over time. One sorry every day will cause a character's confidence to hit a critical low, thus making missions nearly impossible to succeed.

Next time your character feels the itch to say sorry, pause and resist. Depending on the situation, replace the phrase with an optimistic saying. If your character shows up late for a mission, do NOT say sorry, instead say something like, "Thanks for waiting." If your character makes a mistake in a mission, don't tell the crew sorry, instead say "I'll do better on the next one." Here's a quick in-mission example:

A character named Maverick joins a sand volleyball mission. Maverick decides he is the worst one on the court, without any evidence. The ball comes to Maverick and he bumps the ball out of bounds. Last week Maverick had the same instance occur, then instantly said "Sorry." Maverick ended up losing both the game and his confidence. This time around, Maverick remembers the cheat code after making the error, then says "I'll do better on the next one." Now the character's confidence went up instead of down allowing Maverick to build on that confidence, giving him a successful mission.

Next time your character is in a situation that causes a reflex reaction to exalt "sorry," think twice and either don't say anything at all or replace the word with a positive phrase. This cheat code will slowly change a character's confidence bar. Over time, their confidence will be in the green, making them hard to beat and increasing the success odds for any mission.

CHEAT CODE #36: CATCH A VIBE

How is your character's overall aura feeling? If your character's inner state could be associated with a color, what color would it be? Happily yellow? Sadly gray? Possibly a chill navy blue with a slight white tint? No matter how your character is feeling in this moment, their aura or in other words "Vibe" can be changed. Every feeling has a different benefit, yet like anything in the Earth game, too much of anything can damage an avatar.

Characters that experience a healthy amount of gray vibes, allow them to amplify the yellow vibe's happy feelings. On the contrary, an avatar experiencing too many yellow vibes will dampen the stat boosts that the happy feelings provide. Depending on the mission a character hopes to accomplish, getting in the correct vibe mindset is important. If a Player hopes to have their character win a volleyball tournament, the Player could choose to bring their character to a location that in the past has given them confidence. For instance, a character could have felt confident after doing a solo volleyball practice in the park down the street during a previous season. Remembering this feeling of confidence vibe occurring in this location can drastically boost this avatar's confidence levels which will enhance their abilities to be successful in the volleyball tournament.

Catching a vibe is different for each character. The most important aspect of this cheat code is to be aware of your avatar's inner feelings when interacting in different locations or circumstances. Try to constantly take note of a situation to see what exact vibe your character experienced. Then in the future, you'll be able to use the "Catch a Vibe" cheat code to your character's advantage.

Remembering where or what environment made a character feel a certain vibe can be difficult. In order to utilize this cheat code to the fullest, there is one extra step to deepen the effects of the stat-boosting powers. Although simply keeping the character's vibes in a memory storage is better than not being aware at all, actively taking quick notes on where a vibe took place and what kind of vibe happened is critical. Instead of trying to pull thoughts out of an ever-forgetting mind, slowly build a database of how to catch a certain vibe by writing down information on a notes page in the character's phone.

Every time your character experiences a different color feeling or "Vibe", take a few seconds to go into the notes page and write down (Note's header being "Catch a Vibe"): Location, color feeling, and emotion. These three simple details will allow your character to reflect back on the notes page if they are hoping to shift from one mindset's feelings to a whole different vibe. For example, imagine a character named Sparky noticing a unique creative vibe while taking a drive down the freeway. Sparky will then go into their notes page and write: Driving on the freeway, light purple, and creative. Next time Sparky is hoping to shift his mindset to be more creative, he'll go into the notes page, notice he has a specific way to catch the creative vibe, then will proceed to take a drive on the freeway when in need of inspiration.

The location and experience that will cause your character to catch a certain vibe will vastly or slightly differ from other avatars in the game. Since this is the case, constantly be aware of how your character feels during different situations. To increase the chances of finding different places to catch a vibe, have your character often explore and talk with other characters about places that bring them into certain mindsets. Start being aware of places that help your character catch a vibe or your character will struggle to catch new badges.

CHEAT CODE #37: PACE

How are avatars capable of finishing the long-distance run mission called a "Marathon." Maybe they hold the sprint button the whole time? Maybe they refuse to refuel their health with water and food? Absolutely not. Doing this will cause the character to collapse, lose confidence points, and cause a critical hit to the health. So, how are marathons finished successfully? By setting a sustainable pace.

A sustainable pace is when an avatar decides to choose a movement speed that can be maintained over time, without taking a severe depletion of energy to the health/stamina bar. Slowly depleting a character's health, then refueling with water and food, allows characters to persist over long journeys. Before allowing a character's stamina bar to reach red, the avatar needs to take a break in order to rejuvenate the health back to pace ready. After a marathon mission is complete, Players often want to try again with a better time. The Earth game has been coded to reward those Players that give their character a break between missions. Rather than jumping the gun and entering into the next marathon within twenty-four hours, characters will receive a health/overall stats boost by deciding to wait longer than two weeks. Two weeks or more is for a marathon mission, although this Pace cheat code simply explains to set a sustainable pace in every facet of the game. For a minor one-mile run mission, taking two days to recover before the next mission is the status quo. For other missions, for instance, working on a "painting a house" mission, pacing the character to only work four to five hours a day will help prevent the character from taking a critical hit to the health bar.

Taking a critical hit to the health bar, whether on the physical or mental plane, is what the "Pace" cheat code strives to prevent. When you have a chance take a look at how often your character is accepting missions. Are they joining one to two missions a day or three or more missions daily? Doing too many missions in a single login will stop XP from being accumulated. The XP will start to reduce if a Player does not become aware of the overdose of missions.

Next time you log in to the game, look at the missions capable of completing. Choose one, maybe two missions to complete in a day. Disregard the other missions, thus putting 100% focus into the mission(s) at hand. Finish the mission with full effort, then log out. Rest the character after doing a mission. Although the character appears to have plenty of available energy to accomplish other missions, be strong enough to know when to take a break. Instead of doing that extra mission today with 60% health remaining, log out, recover, and join the mission tomorrow with 100% health.

The Earth game can be accessed by one character for many years. There is plenty of time to join thousands of missions over a character's career. Playing the Earth game requires characters to set a pace throughout their game time in order to reach top-tier levels. Setting these sustainable paces will boost XP and the success rate of missions in the long run. Next time you think your character should try to force one more mission in during the day, log out instead and join the mission tomorrow with full health.

CHAPTER 8

CHEAT CODE #38: ONLY SPEAK COMPLIMENTS

Only say positive comments about others. When talking to other team members or characters, remain aware of the words coming out of your avatar's mouth. Regurgitating drama and gossip have been designed in the game to be an easy conversation starter. Spreading negative thoughts about characters has an instant satisfaction, yet drains the social acceptance rating significantly. Not only is XP dropped slightly with every insult spoken behind another Player's back, but eventually that comment makes its way to the character being spoken about.

The Dev team created two options, which can be explained metaphorically. Since mental rewards are harder to imagine than physical rewards, let's walk through a comparative example. Imagine a level two character with a sweet tooth. In this experiment, the noob has the option to receive one piece of candy now or wait an hour for a larger reward of ten pieces of candy. Seeing the importance of patience, level two avatars typically will wait an hour for the twenty pieces of candy. Similarly, would you rather have your character speak poorly about other avatars for instant gratification or speak positively and in a few hours or days receive an XP social ratings boost?

Every character is typically over 90% "good". Rather than talking about the 1-10% of negativity generated by another avatar, decide to think about their qualities and choose to dialogue a compliment. Here's a simple scenario. Two avatars share a headquarters named Stan and Celia. Celia cleans, helps wash wardrobes, and remains quiet often. One day, Celia accidentally leaves music on too loud behind a locked door, which irritates her roommate Stan. Stan, later that day, is with a mutual friend named Karly. Stan thinks about criticizing Celia to Karly by explaining the loud music annoyance. Remembering this cheat code, Stan decides to share with Karly that Celia is a wonderful roommate by being clean. Compliments and criticisms always make it back to the rightful owner. A few days later, Karly tells Celia that Stan said she is a wonderful roommate. Celia now feels loved and is more inclined to remain and improve upon her roommateability.

Remember, the Admin wanted to make the Earth game difficult. This game would be boring if everyone leveled up easily. Use this cheat code to level up quicker and start making more long-term friends. Next time you want to have your character say something negative about another person think about the vast amount of compliments that can be said instead.

CHEAT CODE #39: DON'T KISS AND TELL

Myths grow by themselves. Secrecy creates a fascinating mystery. Accomplishments have a shelf life and a varying impact on a character's XP. Spilling the beans about badges, missions completed or any kind of accomplishment causes the XP boost to decrease. With each

Player you tell your accomplishment to, the XP from that accomplishment diminishes. The goal of this cheat code is to keep your Player's accomplishments out of your avatar's mouth. Achieving XP from successfully finishing a mission will always occur, yet few Players understand that XP for a mission can be increased or decreased even after receiving a badge.

The goal of this cheat code is to increase the amount of XP a character can receive from a mission to its fullest. Each mission's stats can boost or diminish by 25% in either direction. For instance, if a character accomplishes a mission worth an initial payout of 20 XP points, if done correctly those points can go to 25 XP points. If done incorrectly will cause the points to drop to 15 XP. Let's discuss how to receive the 25% increase.

After finishing a mission, a Player needs to keep her character quiet about the accomplishment or speak about the mission in a humble manner by downplaying the significance. Speaking about your own avatar's accomplishments, even to your own team, creates a sense of resentment and envy. Other team members would prefer not to feel this emotion, yet the Admin incorporated this code anyways. Typically another Player will see your accomplishment, then spread positive gossip. Since a separate character passes your accomplishment along to others, each person they tell will boost your character's XP without your Player even realizing how many people have been told. Stay quiet and let other avatars spread your mission accomplishments. Let's walk through what this could look like.

A character named Ang goes on a mission to sing at an open mic. Ang goes up on stage and performs his favorite song to a dull crowd. Ang successfully exhibits genuine energy on stage and has the whole crowd singing along. Ang bows to the crowd, says thank you, and goes home. His XP goes up by 20 XP initially. Ang realizes his accomplishment and wants to tell all his team members about how he excelled at an open mic. Instead of telling them, Ang decides to act like everything is normal. He logs in the next day to explore the local map and none of his team members know about yesterday's performance. Then an avatar in the crowd at open mic, tells everyone how electrifying Ang was the other night. Pleading to everyone about how they missed out on a performance of a lifetime. After a couple of hours, word spreads and team members come up to Ang to boast about his accomplishments to him. Ang humbly acknowledges the successful mission, then continues on with the day. This gave Ang a perfect XP boost of 25.

Next time your character receives a badge from small to large, keep quiet. Don't kiss and tell. Be patient and watch how the word spreads organically, causing your character to receive XP bonuses rather than bragging about your performance, thus reducing the amount of XP that your Player can receive.

CHEAT CODE #40: TALK WITH EVERYONE

What is the easiest way to find treasures or helpful hints? Every character in the game including your own character is full of experience and intellectual gifts to give away to each other to increase the ability to accomplish missions. Spawning new ideas in a character only happens a few times a day and typically the Dev team has the context of those different ideas be similar to the character's recent experiences. But what if your character has plateaued on their current mission's boosts? This is where the talking with everyone cheat code comes into play.

The person on the side of the street has a little gem of knowledge to offer. The clerk working at the health store consists of ideas to propel your character forward in levels. Each one of your team members holds countless pieces of advice to input into your character's mind that will instantly increase their XP and provide the next clue to help continue solving current problems. These thoughts and conversations with any avatar in the game help knock down the point of entry to different missions and badges. Instead of waiting for a rogue thought to enter into your character's mind to be the first building block to a mission's big wall, talk with other avatars and they'll help your character receive 10% - 40% of a mission knowledge needed to acquire the completion badge within minutes of conversation.

The steps to accomplish this cheat code are as simple as walking up to any character and asking them questions then listening intently while proceeding to ask follow-up questions. There are two parts to a conversation, listening and talking. The Dev team developed the characters to have the default setting of preferring talking instead of listening. To perform this cheat code, go into your character's settings and toggle the preferred talking style to listening. Doing this will allow this cheat code to be fully equipped. Listen to any character in the game and they'll automatically provide small to large pieces of hints and treasures that your character can add to their own inventory of knowledge.

The Admin coded this cheat code to reward those Players who allow their character to go out and mingle with more characters. This also will increase the amount of fun in the game by getting characters out of their headquarters and interacting with the world.

In order to visualize this cheat code, let's walk through a quick example. Imagine a character named Coop that is comfortable with staying in their headquarters and prefers to stay away from most interactions with other avatars outside. By being antisocial, Coop is leveling up at an extremely slow pace due to the lack of trying new missions because he isn't able to get advice from others on how to go about getting involved with new missions. Coop decides to try this new cheat code out. He walks outside, goes to a park, sees a person sitting on a bench, then asks if he could sit next to them. Coop asks them "What kind of missions do you like to work towards." The character in the park begins explaining everything they know about learning how to do yoga. Coop learns that getting started in yoga is as simple as going to a free trial class and the other yogis are welcoming and love newcomers. Coop takes a liking to doing yoga which not only gives him a new level up skill from yoga but allows him to meet more people to continue to talk with, receive more advice and learn little treasures from their minds.

Instead of staying indoors and waiting for new ideas and plans to come to your character's mind, go out into the world then begin talking with any avatar. Every character has something to offer that will without a doubt help boost your character's level and XP. Who knows, your character might just meet a character that will end up being their next mission partner for seasons to come.

CHEAT CODE #41: ENERGY PARADOX

Paradox, when a situation appears to be true, yet proves to be the opposite. Plenty of these paradox Easter Eggs were gently scattered throughout the Earth game. Frustrating, sometimes they can be. Converted correctly using cheat codes, paradoxes can be a Player's best friend. Numerous paradoxes exist in this vast game, yet today we focus on the energy paradox.

How does a character drain energy? Using the body for physical activity. Yes and no. How does a character gain energy? Resting the body. Yes and no. Both of these concepts are correct and false at the same time depending on the amount of exertion or relaxation. If done correctly, these statements activate a simple script of code to produce a clear if-then statement. This is a cheat code that relies on reading between the lines.

Moving the character's body for 20 minutes to an hour is equivalent to the purest form of an energy-inducing input. Over-exerting will reduce energy, but doing 20 minutes to an hour worth of movement with the avatar will generate a statement inside the code allowing for this massive energy boost. The clarity, mental health, and most importantly for productivity, energy stat will receive superior enhancements with zero harmful effects (Unless injured during the exercise). Typically, the common Player assumes that applying the character's health to physical activity causes a reduction in overall energy, this is the paradox since it's false and exhibits the opposite effect. The Dev team created this feature to incentivize Players to participate in more activities. When your character is feeling low energy, use the remaining energy to move the body around which catalyzes the avatar to gain sufficient energy to enjoy a productive day.

Here is an example to visualize this odd paradoxical beauty. A character named Zion has 30 out of 100 on the energy bar. He has a mission coming up in a few hours and assumes that he should relax up until the start of the mission. Doing this will give a +10 boost in energy. Zion remembers researching new cheat codes and stumbles across the Energy Paradox. He is skeptical but does not have much of a choice because his next mission needs at least 50% energy for a relevant success rate. Zion decides to get out of the headquarters and slowly jogs around the map for 20 minutes. After finishing this activity, Zion returns to the headquarters and checks the energy level to his disbelief. 75 out of 100 displays on his screen. Zion would later attend the difficult mission with a successful outcome.

Next time your character is feeling sluggish, stand up and start moving the body for a minimum of 20 minutes or a maximum of one hour. If you do not believe this cheat code works, try it for yourself next time there is a log-in day with an easy mission scheduled. You will see the magic before your character's very eyes.

CHEAT CODE #42: NEGATIVES ARE POSITIVES

Worst case scenario, the worst case scenario can be reperspectived into the best case scenario. One painful moment in the Earth game weighs on our characters the same amount as ten delightful moments. Why the Admin did this ratio is yet to be discovered. Perhaps it was a simple error by establishing the variables with an extra zero for the positive effects. Although in some cheat codes, the Admin explain the purpose behind them, then in other circumstances like this cheat code the reason is unknown. Not knowing the reasoning behind the purpose is okay because we can combat the side effects of negatives by reversing their power variable with that of a positive moment's power.

Since a positive moment is worth a +1 on the contentment stats while a negative moment is worth -10 the cheat code that was discovered explains the ability to convert the negative moment from a -10 to a positive moment of +1. In order to do so, the character has two minutes to mentally convert the negative moment into a positive. Some characters have referenced this hack as "Finding the Silver Lining." Every situation no matter how devastating has a chance to be converted. The only difference in the likelihood of reversing the effects to positive is the difficulty of the moment on the character's mind. The more difficult the moment is, the foggier the avatar's mind will be to conjure up a reason the moment can be used as a positive.

Hitting the peak strength of this cheat code requires some creative thinking done by the Player. To receive the base-level benefits of this cheat code, here is the input to type into your character's mind before those two minutes have expired: "I will learn from this moment." Some characters have found an extra amount of benefit on top of this base level by repeating the phrase 1-5 times in those two minutes.

Turn on your character's thinking cap for a few seconds to enhance the strength ability of this cheat code. Depending on your character's situation, think about how the situation could be seen as a positive. Possibly your character's tire popped during a mission. In this situation, your character can feel sorry for themselves and experience the full -10 point hit to their stats or they can turn it around with inputs like these:

- "Maybe if my tire didn't pop, I would have been in a car crash up ahead."
- "Now that my tire has popped, I have the chance to learn about how to change a tire."
- "This popped tire is giving me a break and a legitimate excuse from my mission that was causing me a lot of anxiety."

Whatever the positive phrase may be, anything is better than allowing the character to take hold of a negative thought. By converting the negative into a positive, your character will build strength over time in this cheat code. Soon it will become muscle memory and will require less brain power and creativity from the avatar. Instead, they will be accustomed to saying these quick phrases during a negative moment and making it positive. This will help their day stay on track allowing the character to level up quicker.

A brisk smile changes everything. Character's thoughts come and go. Quickly avatars forget about the previous moments. The memory storage for characters was constructed in an odd way, as opposed to other video games. Rather than the moments in the game constantly being saved with perfect clarity of the moments, the Earth game was developed in a way that reduces the effectiveness for the storage of memory. After playing the game, you'll notice that trying to playback moments from even a few hours ago are foggy. Both with what the scenario visually looked like and the audio. For better or for worse, the avatar's mental health is easily manipulatable. Visually seeing a frown pointed in our character's direction, can easily cause a reduction in the mental health rating.

A simple frown can cause a reduction in the mental health rating, but what is the opposite of a frown? A smile! Seeing someone smile has an instant boost to numerous ratings for our character, but what if your character does not run into smiling avatars often? Great news! The point of this cheat code is not to go out on the map to see other characters smiling at you. This is a smiling code that can be inputted for an instant ratings boost at any moment. In the morning, afternoon, or night, you can have your character do this cheat code for an instant +10 mental health boost. All you have to do is… have your character smile by themselves for five seconds. That simple. Characters typically display a facial expression of neutrality. To make your avatar instantly feel better mentally, make both sides of their mouth rise up to form a smile, hold it there for 5 seconds.

Doing this cheat code results in an instant boost to the mental health rating and remains elated for 30 minutes. A wonderful aspect of this input is that it can be used an unlimited amount of times.

There are no diminishing effects to the code, instead, the more often the Player decides to use this code the longer-lasting the positive effects will remain. Use this simple discovery throughout the game. If your avatar is suffering from a low mental health rating, use it. If they feel neutral, use it. If their health rating is already glowing, use it. The more your character smiles or sees smiling faces, the better.

CHAPTER 9

CHEAT CODE #44: MESS UP LESS

Completing missions will earn your character more XP, and doing nothing will earn your character zero or slightly reduce XP, making mistakes will cause critical damage to your avatar and their XP. Constantly messing up in missions, socially, or financially are quick ways to drop in levels. Sometimes mistakes can even go unnoticed and cause characters to lower in levels with a Player feeling baffled about what's causing their character to demote and lower in stats.

Making mistakes in the social scene is often the most overseen aspect of the Earth game that causes critical hits to stats and XP. Being rude, insulting, frowning, and more toxic mannerisms towards other characters are all ways to reduce your character's overall level. Each social mistake can snowball and drop your character's stats. Be rude to other avatars and other avatars will be rude to your character. The way you treat others will be a reflection of how others will treat you. This cheat code is not so much explaining to be better socially, yet to make fewer mistakes socially. Reducing the number of times your character is rude is similar to a runner taking off a weighted vest.

Now the runner can run freely instead of holding themselves back with all that weight on their shoulders.

On the mission aspect of this cheat code, a Player can enhance their character's leveling-up ability by making fewer mistakes on missions. If a Player wanted to take their character on a trip to a different location on the map by taking an airplane, there are plenty of ways to make the trip worse. By reducing the mistakes, the trip can go smoothly, although often characters will step on their own feet. Instead of showing up to the airport early, characters will lower their XP and increase their stress levels by showing up late and risk missing their flights. This cheat code explains to make fewer mistakes, so in this situation, just go to the airport early to avoid any damage dealt.

The most noticeable area where characters will make mistakes repetitively is finances. Players have their characters mindlessly spend excess tokens on going out to eat, overpaying for items, or even making poor investments through stocks or alternative currencies. Deciding to stay away from spending money poorly or staying out of risky investments will help prevent a character's XP from reducing and stats from taking damage.

Players can become over-focused on completing missions to boost their XP and leveling up, but forget to notice numerous ways they are holding their characters back through mistakes. Often check your character's recent decisions and notice the areas where they are making mistakes. Minimize those mistakes and watch your character run like they just had a fifty-pound vest taken off their body.

Moderation keeps your favorites favorable. Too much of anything is bad and will ruin what was once amazing. If your character finds a certain activity enjoyable with big boosts in any stat, notice the benefits and regulate the interaction with that activity or item. Has your character ever heard a song that quenched their ears so well that you decided to play that song over and over again to the point that the character grew to dislike this once enjoyable tune? This same effect happens throughout the game. Earth is coded in a way that causes the characters to lose interest in what was once adored if the Player is not able to moderate the interactions.

The Admin is said to have created these inputs to prevent an avatar from settling down and repeating a few missions, activities, or items which would hinder the character from exploring what the rest of the Earth game has to offer. Although a character is capable of losing XP from doing an in-game activity too often, the Developers also made Earth reward those Players who can show restraint and do their favorite moments occasionally. The characters are rewarded with around the same XP the following times as the first time if there is a large enough time window between these activities.

Many characters will overdo simple pleasures most commonly. For example: drinking coffee too regularly, playing sports every single day, hanging out with the same character all the time, repeatedly doing the same mission, playing arcade games, partaking in character-altering items, and much more. All of these, depending on the character, are good in moderation. Moderation is making sure not to do a certain in-game activity too frequently. Instead of drinking coffee every day, drink coffee once every three days. Drinking coffee every day will reduce the energy-boosting effects.

Although, if consumed irregularly, the character's body will regularly boost energy in a way that is helpful for the avatar. Thus, giving the character power to fulfill more missions after drinking the coffee.

Let's see what an example of this moderation might look like. Imagine there is a character in the Earth game named Chief. Chief has numerous missions to complete across a wide range of categories. One day, Chief would like to be on the Top 1000 leaderboard charts. A new arcade game comes out to play inside of Earth and Chief takes a liking to it so much that he decides to spend all playing hours on the arcade game instead of missions. Chief's team gets worried about his newfound addiction to an activity reducing XP instead of improving rank. The team member Willow finds this "Moderation" cheat code, then presents it to Chief. He instantly inputs the cheat code and now only plays the arcade game every couple of days for a limited amount of time. Thanks to Willow, Chief is back on track to reaching the Top 1000 in the next few seasons.

As we see in this example, excess admiration for any activity, even if the XP was boosted in the beginning significantly, can quickly lower the rank of a character. Have awareness of your character. Notice their tendencies and act sooner than later. The later a Player waits to change an avatar's addiction, the harder it will be to stop. Use the "Moderation" cheat code early on for every little activity and enjoy preserving some of your character's favorite activities.

CHEAT CODE #46: OSMOSIS

Characters that are in the same proximity of each other, communicate over the text chat or on the mic, automatically will develop their stats. Simply by interacting with other characters in the game will constantly change many different categories of your avatar's abilities.

Since the fluctuation of the character's stats happens automatically, the avatar can become better or worse automatically. Hence, if a Player is not careful with who their character is surrounding themselves with can easily lower a character's stats quickly. Although, if a Player knows this cheat code, they will be able to naturally boost their XP and abilities just by spending time with quality characters.

Depending on where a Player chooses their character to start their journey can determine the number of potential quality friends. If there are few options to meet quality characters whose goals are to complete missions, then have your character spend more time alone until a high-quality friend comes around. The Dev team decided to reward those Players with extra XP who choose a difficult location to start their journey and still can develop quality friendships.

Let's take a look at the two different options for friendship which causes learning and stat development through osmosis. A character that decides to give in to their lonely feelings and make friends with characters that are constantly leveling down will cause your character's motivation and determination levels to drop. If your character hangs out with them long enough, your character will also begin dropping in levels automatically. On the flip side, if your character decides to wait until a quality friend comes around, then that new friend will boost your avatar's motivation and determination levels. With these categories of stats increasing will automatically cause your character to level up quickly.

Be careful who your character is spending time with. Are these other characters leveling up or becoming worse at the Earth game? If they are becoming worse, then understand that your character too, is becoming worse simply by being near or communicating with them. Spend time alone because eventually a quality friend will come around and your characters will begin to develop together.

Keep your character's badges page on private mode. Automatically the Devs coded the OS to cause avatars to have their badges page public. The Admin explained the purpose for doing this, on a hidden forum, was to hinder the majority of characters from leveling up. If everyone was capable of leveling up then being a higher level would not be as important. Leveling up was designed to be difficult, that way a small portion of avatars rise through the leaderboards. Earth is a sandbox-style game. Interestingly, the updates and new seasons are guided by what Players decide to create. The Admins provide their new input to the game infrequently and leave the majority of the game for the Players to decide the outcome. The Players working towards having their character be humble have a better chance of receiving new ideas to their random thought list.

Next time your character finishes a mission or receives a badge, keep quiet. Don't inject your avatar's accomplishments into a conversation. This will reduce the XP points that were already received, even if the points came from many days ago. Instead of spontaneously discussing the avatar's badges or success, wait for another Player to ask about your badges. Doing this cheat code boosts your character's XP and different ratings, for example: humility. Remaining humble and not boasting about accomplishments enhances a character's overall stat quickly. Now that another Player knows about your accomplishments, they will spread your badges all while keeping your character's humility rating high.

Another way for this cheat code to be activated is by having witnesses of your success spread the word. If Players spread your successful moments from a first-hand account, the XP is that much greater. After having a positive mission with other characters nearby, be sure to stay calm and humble in the moment as well. Displaying overconfidence or bragging during a successful mission will cause a reduction in the social rating. Characters are inherently developed to feel distaste towards a braggadocio, although experience an affinity towards those who act casual after success.

Next time your character wins or performs with skill, keep a calm expression. Look like the character is used to these actions. XP will be boosted instantly and then increased again every time another Player discusses your accomplishments without your character discussing it themselves randomly. Keep quiet!

CHEAT CODE #48: SMALL WINDOW

"Dude you are not very good at accomplishing missions. I'm not even sure why I hang out with you. Just leave the game." Remarks like these happen throughout the game every day. Users that continually insult other Players in the Earth game receive the bully badge connected to their account. Even though having the bully badge associated with their account, these types of characters continually cause harm. Having the bully badge will slowly reduce their friendship capabilities, but this is not a cheat code to help bullies remove their badge. Instead, this is a cheat code that shows the strategy to receive one of the top five biggest XP boosts in the game.

Often, a bully will insult another avatar in the presence of no one else, yet some bullies will be so confident in their insults that at certain moments they will insult a character close enough to another Player watching. This moment creates a small window for the third-party Player to decide to defend the recipient or stay silent. Staying silent, according to the Developers' code, shows zero reduction in the character's XP, which is odd but maybe that's just how the game is currently coded. Reacting before thirty seconds have elapsed in a way to bring comfort to the receiver of harm will give a character a 100 XP boost! According to the documents I'm reading, the Developers had a big meeting with the whole staff to determine how much of a helpful reaction a Player needs to perform to receive the full XP boost and declared that even the smallest amount of help will receive all 100 XP.

There are numerous ways to help another character getting bullied or harmed. These situations vary depending on the situation and it is recommended to go about helping in the safest way possible to avoid harm to your own character. During a verbal insult, your character can either explain to the bully that their actions of harm are not okay, tell the bully to stop with the insults and leave, and then comfort the user receiving the harm.

In a physical confrontation, help the character being harmed the most your character is capable or comfortable with. Maybe your character is a high level with stats in the strength category exceeding the bullies, in this scenario maybe interject. At the minimum tell the bully to stop their actions and call for help.

There are numerous ways to handle these small-window situations. The Admin decided to make the XP boost so large because these situations are by far one of the most difficult situations to react in. Growing the courage in your character to help defend against a bully requires a lot of skill, but if your character is capable of making a move to interject and stop a bully in their tracks the Admin will reward your character greatly. Incorporating this cheat code, according to the Admin, will allow for a safer Earth game and will greatly reward those characters who are capable of kindness in frightening situations.

The Earth game is quite interesting. Unlike most video games, the eating and drinking aspect of the Earth game plays a major factor in what the character inputs into the body. Most games allow avatars to consume a few different options for improving the health bar with straightforward results. For instance, in the majority of video games a character eats an apple and the health bar boosts by +5. In the Earth game, a Player has the chance to choose what the character can eat amongst thousands of options, with each option having different effects to separate portions of the avatar's stats.

In the Earth game, a character can consume an apple and receive +5 to the health bar, although that apple will have a ripple effect across different stats like mental clarity, creativity, energy, and so on. The quality of the apple matters as well. Apples that were grown in poor environments could cause the health bar to go negative. Also, unlike most games, food in the Earth game can become spoiled, which if eaten will make the character sick causing severe damage. In the Earth game, especially in these newer seasons with the implementation of farming, making a character "full" and not hungry is simpler than ever. Finding food is easier than ever, yet during these recent seasons, the characters are more unhealthy now than ever. This is due to the access to low-quality food which is detrimental to a character's overall stats.

The characters in the game "are what they eat." The most sophisticated code ever developed was created for the Earth game. Every time a character eats or drinks, the body breaks down the material and uses those pieces of the food to repair and continually generate the character's body. If a character eats fast food hamburgers only, then the body is going to break down those hamburgers into tiny pieces and replace the body with greasy materials. Although, if a character eats healthy food then the character's body will repair and fuel the body with quality material, thus allowing the avatar to increase its success rate during missions.

This cheat code explains the need for Players to discover healthy foods and consistently have their character consume high-quality material, as opposed to health-reducing food. The Admin decided to make eating healthy slightly more difficult than eating low-quality food. In the Earth game, Players have the option to shop at grocery stores. All grocery stores have healthy foods to improve a character's overall health, although these stores also have foods that are harmful to characters but are constantly purchased due to the low prices. Characters can either go to a regular grocery store and find healthy food or another option is to shop at a grocery store known for only stocking quality foods.

Eating healthy costs more money by typically 20%, but this extra investment in your character's body is the best investment a Player can make according to the Dev team. Purchasing food that is 20% more expensive will improve a character's overall level by 40% over time. Before going to the store, research 2-5 healthy meals. Bring the exact ingredients list to the store which sells these kinds of food and purchase them. Watch the magic of eating properly work for itself, within a few days your character's stats will increase dramatically.

Eating quality food will give your avatar more energy, think more clearly, and make them more productive. Then by being more productive, the character can complete more missions which will allow them to collect more tokens, thus being capable of affording these recommended higher-quality foods. Next time your character is ready to fill their stomachs, pause and find food that is healthy even if the food costs more tokens. In the end your character will earn more than they spent on the healthy food.

CHAPTER 10

CHEAT CODE #50: SAVE MORE MAKE MORE

One way to accumulate more tokens in the Earth game is by not spending as many tokens in the first place. Crazy concept, I know. So easy, yet so hard to do in reality. From saving a few tokens on a purchase, to not making unnecessary big purchases. Being aware of how your character is using their tokens will allow your character to make more tokens. Instead of spending tokens in the first place, this cheat code simply explains, to use fewer tokens. According to the Dev team, everything in the Earth game can be purchased for less if the user checks the price at numerous stores or tries to get a second or third opinion on services. Businesses in the game are designed to ask for the highest amount of tokens from characters. Not only to make the businesses money but to constantly test the characters to see if they will choose to save tokens or mindlessly waste funds.

Aside from spending fewer tokens during purchases, the second option to save more is to sell off overpriced items that your character already has in their possession. Possibly, your character has too many high-end clothes that they rarely wear? Use a selling app or website to sell them off. Maybe your avatar has a car that is worth more than it's worth in happiness. Sell it! Then find a cheaper transportation vehicle or method. Does your character have a headquarters that is too expensive or big for what they need? Sell it and move to a different location that suits your character's needs perfectly. A difficult expense to track, which slowly drains Players' token amount are subscriptions. Double-check across all of your token accounts that you are solely subscribed to businesses that you intend to be paying.

Doing all of these savings techniques will save your character plenty of tokens while increasing their XP as well. Then with higher XP, leveling up, and more tokens in their account, the character might be wise enough to use those extra tokens to make more tokens. With fewer expenses, your character can live with less stress and more peace thus allowing the happiness stat to boost significantly. You will never find out how helpful saving tokens can be for your character until you have them begin to cut back on expenses and start saving!

CHEAT CODE #51: INVEST IN YOURSELF

Buy this stock and you'll 10x your tokens within days! Give us your tokens today and we'll put them towards different businesses that will make you more tokens. Use your precious time and work for us for the majority of the day then finish the game day so tired that you won't have enough energy to finish missions that you enjoy. The Earth game has created numerous distractions to pry characters away from believing in themselves. The direction the majority of Players decide to take is the simplest one. "Hi there rookie, work for me and do as I say, you'll be comfortable and your work will make me money so that I don't have to work." Every character has the capability to produce creative thoughts that will fuel their missions with sufficient tokens and the ability to have a surplus of tokens if they stay consistent.

Investing in yourself can take many different forms. From the most common occurrences like eating to the boldest circumstances like putting all your character's tokens towards creating a main stream of income that can solely fuel paying for the character's basic needs to continue playing. When I found this cheat code in the Admins' lock box, there was a small side note that said "For those Players that decide to, in any form, invest in themselves their stats will exponentially increase in certain areas which will allow them to stay consistent more easily the longer their streak is in a particular area of the game." This basically means that if your plan is to invest in having your character eat healthier foods rather than junk food, not only will your stats continue to boost in the health section, but the likelihood of your character wanting to eat healthy increases which will allow them to stay consistent for the long haul.

If your character decides they want to be bold and begin slowly separating themselves from their work and create a form of income that is generated solely off the character's time, the Admin coded the game to reward these actions with stat boosts. Every Player has the ability to decide what to spend their tokens on: disposable items (alcohol, overpriced meals, anything that loses value over time) or investments (properties, businesses, personal skills, anything that increases in value over time). The majority of Players will decide to purchase disposable items for instant gratification, but once the character spends the tokens those tokens are gone forever. However, if a Player decides to have their character spend their tokens towards investing in making their character better, those tokens will pay dividends in the future. Although the tokens are gone now, the Admin determined that those spending tokens on improving their character will be rewarded in the future with more tokens.

Picture a character named Natalie who has earned tokens working with the same company for 15 seasons. Natalie has witnessed other characters on her team become financially independent by creating revenue off of monetizing their hobbies. Natalie thought that investing in herself was selfish and risky causing her to always spend her tokens on the basics to keep the character alive. After finding the "Invest in Yourself" cheat code, Natalie decided to think of a hobby she enjoyed and wondered how to earn tokens from the hobby. She decided she loved rollerblading. Natalie had the idea to rent out rollerblading equipment in a local park and give lessons for a few tokens an hour. She used money from her savings to get the business going through purchasing equipment. After starting the rollerblading rental business in the park she received amazing reviews leading to her business going viral and drawing in characters from all over the map. Due to investing in herself, Natalie triggered the cheat code and allowed her character to increase the odds of success. She now is her own boss and quit her job, which boosted her XP and stats across the emotional board. All simply by taking the "risk" to invest in herself.

Tokens are a big factor in leveling up or down a character. The Earth game incorporated these in order to develop another way of separating the characters in the game depending on their decisions. Those who spend their tokens and time towards improving their character's skills will be rewarded in the future. Those characters that can stay consistent with investing in themselves over numerous seasons will eventually find themselves in a position where they look back on their decisions and are amazed at how far they have come. Simply speaking, invest in yourself and limitlessly level up your character.

CHEAT CODE #52: GO PLAY TODAY

Want to go play today? Play? The same way beginner characters do? Yes, that same kind of play. Have you ever gone to the leaderboard to see which avatars have the highest ratings for joy? Levels 1-12 have an average rating of 90 for joy. High-level characters throughout the game have referred to this phenomenon as having a beginner's mind or a child-like mind. There are numerous reasons for this occurrence, yet one that stands out is the fact that low-level characters enjoy going out and "playing." Playing in the playful sense. Doing activities with little expectations. Deciding to, by oneself or with friends, choose an enjoyable mission just for the fun of the experience.

Low-level characters do not realize that these activities are helping them level up and increase their joy rating significantly. By doing these missions, the Players are having their avatars move their bodies around, which also boosts strength, endurance, and mental health ratings. The goal of this cheat code is to have your character play anything for sixty minutes a day. The playful activity can be anything that causes the reluctant to step outside of a comfort zone to "play" since the stigma is that only lower-level characters should be the ones playing daily. However, the Dev team decided to make this cheat code available to reward those characters willing to risk their serious persona to just go out and play.

Level 1-12 is commonly referred to as the "kid" levels. Time to be a kid again. Paradoxically, deciding to do more lower-level activities will dramatically increase a character's level. What are some examples of playing, you might ask? Here's a list to start with:

- Jogging

- Lifting weights

- Basketball

- Surfing

- Tag

- Capture the Flag

- Volleyball

- Wiffle Ball

- Tennis

- Swimming

- Yoga

- Sharks and Minnows

- Blob

- Frisbee

Pick one of these missions or find a different one, then set a timer on the screen for sixty minutes. Keep playing for the entire period. Afterward, your character will have numerous different categorical rating boosts. Continue this trend daily to witness the power of playing to increase an avatar's joy, physical/mental health, and much more!

CHEAT CODE #53: ONCE A WEEK

Tired of being too tired to build your character's skills? Here is a cheat code that is as simple as sitting down. Why? Because that's exactly what you might be doing during this consistency hack. Consistent? Yes, consistent. This is a productivity code, meaning your character will input this into the Earth game to boost a few character skills, the two main ones are productivity and specific skill enhancement.

Think of something your avatar has always wanted to become better at. Learn a language? Boost character endurance? Music achievements? Increase strength levels? Drawing? Completely up to you! Now listen or read closely to the button-by-button cheat code: Do an activity, of your choice, for 30 minutes once a week on the same day and time. The biggest thing to get this code rolling is to sit down or go to the exact spot where your new leveling-up skill is performed. If it's reading more books. Grab a book and sit down in a quiet place. Your avatar will not know what to do other than start reading. Let's say your name is Sally, now let's create an example for you, Sally. Oh, Sally! I heard through the grapevine you want to become better at drawing. Very interesting. Here's the cheat code in action:

Sally thinks: "I'm going to input the "Once a Week" code. How about every Tuesday at 11 am I will draw for 30 minutes. Because this is usually when I'm awake after some coffee and it's not Monday, so I should have extra energy."

Sally thinking: *Tuesday at 11 am* "Time to draw something! Let me set a timer on my phone for 30 minutes.

Sally: *Draws a tree for 30 minutes enthusiastically then puts the drawing in the drawer to work on next Tuesday at 11 am for 30 minutes*

The hidden code behind this input is that your character begins to be slowly rewired to get used to being more consistent with not only drawing but more aspects of your character's story mode. A way to increase the accuracy of this cheat code is by picking a moment in your day and week when you already know you will be energetic. For instance, after drinking coffee or after getting a workout in. This will help make your character more consistent and it makes the activity more enjoyable! After your character performs this cheat code for a few weeks less willingly, the avatar starts to get used to the routine and will feel an odd sensation if the cheat code is not performed. Then your character will end up craving to do this activity more than once a week. This is a great sign of the cheat code working at a diamond level! Now go out and see how consistent your character can become.

CHEAT CODE #54: BUMP AND DANCE

Feeling down in the dumps or is your character's energy not matching what you were hoping for when you logged in? There are different power-ups a character can purchase with tokens and consume, but there is a free, more clean way to boost happiness. Bump some tunes! Tunes refers to music of course. Whether the goal is to increase excitement levels or feel a certain mood, playing music helps put a Player's avatar in the proper mindset needed to achieve daily goals.

Music in the game is completely free assuming they are connected to the global phone system for accessing the Earth game's knowledge known as the internet. Music and dancing have been the biggest source of entertainment since season one. The Admin planned the hearing sense to provide a spatial visual in the early seasons to avoid danger or to complete important missions like hunting for food. As the characters in the game became better at providing their local groups with more comfort by storing food, playing music and dancing after big accomplishments became a norm in the game's communities.

As the seasons went on, Players continued to advance the development and mass production of music which allows any character to have access to this audible liquid gold. During a recent seasonal update to the Earth game, the Admin decided to enhance the amount of happiness music brings to a character. They even added an extra boost if Players had their avatars get up and groove to the sounds in the form of dancing. The Developers began to enjoy this new form of entertainment called music so much that they changed the code so that listening, dancing, and singing along to the music will easily bring characters out of critically low happiness moments. Doing these actions, according to the Dev team, can pull anyone out of a low-happiness stat without even needing to be genuine with their voluntary activity.

Let's boogie our way through an example of what the "Bump and Dance" cheat code might look like. Envision a character named Bookie who wakes up in the game and feels a sense of dread being produced from a critically low happiness level. Bookie typically will seek entertainment with the hopes of uplifting her mood in the form of social media. Scrolling through her social media content causes the communal comparison effect where characters feel worse about their own situation when noticing others seeming to enjoy their lives. The common post revolves around only showing the avatar's best moments, causing an illusion that all Players are constantly doing successful missions. When in reality each character is experiencing losses, lulls, and success. Being aware of her imminent downward spiral of happiness, Bookie tries the "Bump and Dance" technique. Excited, Bookie picks three songs that she loves, puts headphones in, starts the music, jumps out of bed, and begins singing, dancing, and listening to warming sounds. The code realizes Bookie's inputs and then instantly bounces her mood back into the positive. Bookie with the new and improved happiness levels, feels better about herself and crushes her daily mission goals.

Why not take time to jam out to your character's favorite music? Listening to songs brings instant benefits to avatars no matter what mood they might be experiencing at the moment. Not sure what to play? Look up on a phone the happiest songs of the season and start moving the body and singing along. Enjoy!

CHAPTER 11

CHEAT CODE #55: LET IT OUT

If your character drank poison, would you just have them leave it inside of them? Or would you make the biggest effort for them to regurgitate the foul fluid that entered their body? Unless you're into funny business, surely you would get it out ASAP. Similar to poison, but much more elusive and nearly invisible are poisonous thoughts. Often these thoughts can be more deadly than drinking a dangerous substance. How? Poison has a chance to physically be released from the avatar's body whether that's through forced bodily liquid ejection or seeing an in-game doctor soon enough. Sadly, some thoughts that creep into a character's mind are so vicious that they will convince the mind to self-destruct themselves. Known in the game as suicide.

Depending on your character's initial installed personality will often determine the severity of how deadly these intrusive thoughts can grow into. Nonetheless, all characters throughout the entire game are susceptible to poisonous thoughts that can lead to deadly outcomes whether they are aware this is a possibility or not.

There are numerous cheat codes to prevent mental poison from coming to the point of no return. This cheat code focuses on a healing style that is similar to vomiting a physical poison. Instead of releasing harmful fluids from the body, this cheat code explains the importance of the character letting out harmful thoughts going on in their mind. The two different ways to do this most commonly are: write down the thoughts going on in the character's mind or meet up with a trusty team member that is willing to listen without judgment. The latter is the most effective, although it requires having a strong relationship with another avatar to open up to. Writing down the character's thoughts is easier to fulfill and gives the character some privacy if they are nervous to tell their thoughts to someone. Here are examples of how both options will look in practice.

Writing down your character's thoughts on a piece of paper or a phone allows the Player to physically see what's going on in the brain to determine the severity of the thoughts. Often an avatar will write down their thoughts assuming their mental state is a 10/10 on the damage scale, when in fact by encountering the thoughts in word form they find out that the damage is closer to a 4/10. A character named Victoria was having spooky thoughts. She decided to do this cheat code and let it out on a piece of paper. She wrote "My friends did not text me back quick enough for tonight's mission. Are they upset with me? If I was in their shoes, would I have responded quickly? Possibly they were busy and responded once they were ready to respond." Now that the thoughts are out of Victoria's mind, she is able to develop her fears instead of being on a loop of her assumptions for responding slowly. Forcing herself to write out the different options, creates the ability to see the bright side of the situation once she runs out of pessimism to write. Worst case scenario, this cheat code was included by the Admin who made it so that a character will be rewarded XP and a content stat boost simply for attempting this exercise.

The other option is to do this similar style of mental vomiting by venting to a friend willing to listen. A character named Walt is on a basketball team in the Earth game and was struggling mentally with wondering if the coach was going to play him in the games or not. He decided to talk with his friend and teammate, Riff, about his scary thoughts. Walt explained to Riff "I'm working hard during practice, always positive, and try my best whenever the coach is watching." Riff listens to Walt without judgment and allows Walt to continue to vent. Riff does not provide much advice, just an open ear for their friend Walt to speak to. Walt releases those thoughts from his head, instantly making him be able to see his own thoughts outside his body and slowly getting the mental thought poison away from his own mind. Similar to writing down a character's mental pains, the character will automatically be rewarded a contentment stat boost.

Get those thoughts out of your character's body. Imagine those thoughts to have the same effect as liquid poison. Both poisons require urgent attention. If the thoughts or the liquid are neglected and remain in the character's body, both can have deadly consequences. Next time your character has a lot of pain in their mind, find a lovely friend or blank piece of paper to vomit the thoughts onto and notice the newfound relief.

CHEAT CODE #56: ASSETS OVER LIABILITIES

Over the last sixty seasons of the Earth game, the Admin has reduced the token's buying power by 3.8% yearly on the USA map. Other sandbox locations experience higher than 3.8% while sometimes vastly more and few times less than 3.8%. Tokens sitting in your character's account are reducing in value every moment. One hundred tokens today will be worth ninety-six tokens a season from now. The Dev team does this on purpose. Characters are constantly sending complaint requests to the support email "I work hard on my missions to earn tokens and then if I save them your Earth game reduces the value?!" Their response "If we kept the value of your tokens equal every year, you would not use the tokens often enough."

Inflation is encoded into the game for better or for worse. Thankfully, there are cheat codes to save tokens effectively without losing value every year, and over the long term the tokens will increase in value. There are two types of items that have value in the Earth game: assets and liabilities. Liabilities are items that lose value over time automatically. For example: tokens, food, clothes, computers, vehicles, and so on. Assets are items that increase in value over time automatically. For example: houses, gold, stocks, collectibles, businesses, and so on.

The most common asset that is used as a long-term piggy bank is using your character's tokens for buying a headquarters also known as a house. Over the previous sixty seasons, the value of a house has gone up by 4.2% yearly. At this rate, using tokens to purchase a house will increase your token value by .4% yearly. Rather than losing 3.8% yearly, your character has a safe place to store tokens through an asset and will increase the token value by doing nothing. Not only will your character's token value increase over time through purchasing a house as an asset, but the house can be rented out to other characters to generate revenue for your character to collect monthly. By purchasing a house worth 100,000 tokens can allow your avatar to collect up to 1000 tokens a month without needing to do anything except infrequent maintenance.

The buying assets over liabilities cheat code does not get used often because saving requires long-term thinking which the majority of characters' long-term thinking rating is low. Buying a house is easy, yet feels scary. The scarier something feels, often the greater the reward. Here is an example of a character who decided to buy a house with their tokens instead of allowing the token's value to decrease in their account.

Ziggy saved up 50,000 tokens over missions for a few years. He heard about the cheat code regarding purchasing assets and decided to give it a try. Ziggy came across a house that cost 100,000 tokens. He used 20,000 of his 50,000 tokens to put down on the house and took a 30-season loan out for the remaining 80,000 tokens. The loan cost 800 tokens a month and Ziggy rented the house for the first year at 1000 a month then increased the rent by 4.2% yearly. Fifty to sixty seasons later, Ziggy's house is worth 900,000 tokens and rents for 9000 tokens a month. Ziggy made money with his tokens throughout the years instead of allowing his tokens to decrease in value in his bank account, which happens to the majority of characters.

Instead of allowing your character to constantly purchase liabilities that reduce or completely lose value, have your avatar start thinking about purchasing assets. Making an asset purchase might feel scary at the moment, but after a few years, your character will level up quicker and increase their token value. Buy assets, not liabilities.

CHEAT CODE #57: WASTE YOUR TIME WISELY

There's a character named Fili whose Player always has him skipping missions to intoxicate. Every time the Player logs into the Earth game, He has His character find drugs that make for instant satisfaction, yet inflicts damage across the stat board. Once the drug boost is complete, the comedown occurs and Fili feels worse than when they started. A popular slang term for these reverse missions is called "Getting Wasted." Fili in this scenario constantly wastes his time unwisely. The amount of harm outweighs any benefit that can come from wasting his time. Wasting time unwisely comes in an infinite amount of forms, for example: consuming drugs, doing anything too much, sleeping more than 10 hours, hanging out with other time wasters, and all other activities that lack productivity.

On the other hand, there's a character named Tacti who has adopted this cheat code of "Waste Your Time Wisely." Starting missions does not always bring noticeable rewards. Working towards anything productive like training for different exercise events, making friends, or building businesses, does not always generate success in the standard terms. Working towards any goal can lead to an unwanted end. Training for a marathon and then contracting an illness the day before, might feel like a waste of time. Going to an event to make new friends and coming home with no new friend request approvals, might feel like a waste of time. Spending money to start a business then never going positive on revenue, might feel like a waste of time. These examples might feel like a waste of time because it is a waste of time, but done wisely.

The time spent towards these goals that end up being "failures" cannot be recovered, yet your character has developed skills across their depth chart which might be unseen. Every attempt towards a mission will always boost different stats according to the Admin. As long as the Player attempts to have their character do a mission, no matter how big or small, they will always be rewarded even if they fail or cannot finish. A side note that was on this cheat code in the Admin's office explained by "Wasting Your Time Wisely" will not only increase different skills and abilities but allows the odds of achieving a goal to increase. The Earth game is a numbers game. With every attempt gives the character another roll of the dice. Unlike a casino, the Earth game allows characters to attempt towards any goals as many times as they want. Sometimes if a character makes a business, they will make money off of their first business which is equivalent to rolling a seven on the first attempt at a craps table. Or maybe a character will start five different businesses but loses money until the sixth business. The trick is to continually take attempts and although not achieving the goal will feel like a failure your character has actually succeeded.

Is there a mission in the game that you want your character to try? Start today. Give it an attempt. Start spending time building towards those goals. The odds are you will end up feeling like you wasted your time. If you feel this way, keep trying or take another attempt with a different plan. Either way, keep attempting any mission you would like to see your character finish, and eventually you will roll that lucky number seven and feel the success of winning.

CHEAT CODE #58: NO TOKENS, NO PROBLEM

A character with fewer tokens levels up faster and higher than a character with an overabundance of tokens. Playing the Earth game requires characters to use tokens to participate in certain missions or enhance their appearance. Although tokens can be used as a vehicle to join more missions, many tokens do not always conclude a Player will easily interact with the game to their benefit. Characters holding a high amount of tokens and gloating about their in-game wealth will surprisingly find that their happiness, social stats, and leveling-up abilities are low.

The Admin created the Earth game as a non-profit with the goal of studying the outcome of a society when the power lies in the

Players' hands. The Admin decided to include tokens into the game without making a profit themselves. Tokens play a critical role in the Earth game by generating another skill needed to be learned. If a character understands that tokens are there to pay for more learning, to give away, and to be humble, then they will be the ones that will level up quickly.

The Earth game's construction allows all Players to level up and boost their social and happiness levels without the need for a significant amount of currency. The majority of missions are free or require little tokens to complete. Thanks to high-level tech characters, knowledge and content were made available to the whole game for free as long as they have access to the internet. Due to this, any character has the ability to level up their character through learning. A Player is capable of having their character reach the maximum level solely from free knowledge.

Let's walk through an example of how a Player can level up their character with minimal tokens. Louis joined the game recently and is physically capable to accomplish any mission, yet lacks tokens to join expensive events. Louis hears about the cheat code explaining that characters don't need many tokens to level up due to free or cheap events plus the introduction of the internet for knowledge. Louis decides that he wants to learn how to code video games, but thought college was required to receive the coding badge. Louis decides to go to a local library, logs on to the free computer's internet, and types into the search bar "How to Learn Code for Free." Louis finds a plethora of resources teaching game development code. He chooses one, spends a few months learning, gets a job developing games, and now is in a position to join missions that cost more tokens if need be.

Tokens are not required to level up and play the game with enjoyment. A survey was conducted by the Admin, showing that characters with the lower 50% of the tokens have higher happiness and social stats. Typically characters having more tokens are stressed or find creating genuine friendships difficult. If your character has few tokens, remember that they can enjoy the game just as much as any character in the game. If your character has a significant amount of tokens, remember to stray from flaunting having those tokens, or else having genuine friendships will be more difficult.

CHEAT CODE #59: THRIFT SHOP

In-game purchases are continually increasing in price. Most Players assume that their character needs to accumulate piles of tokens until they can splurge on new outfits for their character. You guessed it, this cheat code explains that's not the case. Have you ever noticed the character's confidence bar after wearing a shirt that the character has never worn before? Significant confidence boost! You might be thinking, "Well I can't use my tokens to buy a new shirt often or I'll go broke." Keyword, "new."

One of the most underrated cheat codes in the whole game of Earth is the thrift shop or second-hand stores! The Admin purposely placed plenty of thrift shops in every city. Some characters will think they are "too good" for used clothes or items. Although, characters that choose to input the "Thrift Shop" cheat code will automatically have their reluctance stats dropped enough to take themselves to a thrift shop with thrill. There are no minimal token requirements to enter a thrift shop. These second-hand stores are made for all Players of the game, from those with boundless badges to those just getting started. A new (to your character) shirt or any other piece of clothing is in the shop waiting for your character to discover. Here's the best part that has been implied but not mentioned yet, the clothes are extremely cheap! Not only are they cheap, but Players will not have to worry about the odd shrinking bug in the game. The clothes being prewashed and already worn makes it so the character will not have to discard the clothes from their inventory after wearing them once. Most new clothes are coded to shrink after being washed for the first time, which causes the character to be forced to wear it with a confidence deduction or remove it from their inventory. Let's walk through this cheat code step by step.

Open the map of your local playground. Type in "thrift shop." Look for a thrift shop that stands out to you. One of the most sought-after thrift shops is called "Good Will." Good Wills have shirts ranging from 3-10 credits! Turn on navigation, then head towards the shop on the map. Walk into the shop, scour the clothes racks, and find a shirt that fits your character nicely and looks good according to you. Purchase the shirt, go back to your headquarters and next time you're on a mission wear your new shirt! The confidence stat will be boosted by +5!

Now that you know this cheat code, feel free to go to thrift shops and buy well-fitting, unique clothes for nearly free!

CHAPTER 12

CHEAT CODE #60: EYE SEE YOU

The most enjoyable food in the game is often the most damaging for a character. Non deadly poison frequently is disguised as being delicious. According to the Admin, characters are attracted to these foods, known as junk food, to give those avatars with self-control a competitive advantage. Ingesting these damaging foods causes numerous stats of a character to drastically decline, for instance: speed, endurance, mental clarity and so much more. The character's body rebuilds with the foods that they eat, which if they eat unhealthy food, they are rebuilding their character's physical body with the equivalence of junk. Although eating healthy food is important, more importantly, is what a character consumes through their eyes and ears.

Similar to food, there are healthy and unhealthy content characters are constantly consuming through visuals and sounds. These two senses are capable of leveling up a character but have the same counter effect to demote an avatar quickly. Without filtering the content being consumed through these senses, a character will obtain an unhealthy mind. The mind is the forerunner for all actions. By choosing to watch videos or listening to conversations that are unproductive or draining, a character's mind will also be diminished. The most common form of unhealthy content being ingested is found in movies, social media platforms, and low-level news stations.

Spending time in these environments instead of completing missions or learning new skills is detrimental to the character's leveling-up abilities. Movies with drama, displaying violence, or promoting unethical behaviors are unconsciously absorbed by a character's mind. Social media and news networks are another form of junk food content that does more harm than benefit. Instead of focusing on spending time listening and watching these forms of content, focus on involving your character with healthy content.

Healthy content changes depending on the character, yet there is a common thread connecting the beneficial content to be involved with. Focus your character's content absorption on learning and positive emotional visuals and audio. Surround the character with content that brings them happiness, for example: art, writing, exercise, reading, or anything that makes a character feel better instead of worse. Choose news networks, movies, and social media that focus on your character's interests which can translate to enhancing skills or happiness.

Characters in the Earth game are hypersensitive to the content they watch or hear. Since this is the case, being aware of what your character sees and listens to is even more important than consciously eating healthy food. Take a moment to realize the different areas of the game your character is involved with then begin cutting out the bad and doubling down on the good.

Will you remember this day in the Earth game next year or will it be a vague memory like most moments in the game? Deep memories are the highest form of a badge a character can obtain. Without strong enjoyable adventurers that create a memory badge, the game lacks meaning. Since the ability to beat the Earth game has yet to be discovered, the next best form of winning is not to constantly level up, but to participate in missions so memorable it turns into a memory badge.

Memory badges are capable of being accomplished every login, although the majority of Players have their character remain stagnant causing missions to go uncomplete. Lack of participation in missions and adventurers prevents this highest form of badge to be achieved. Days without collecting a memory are equivalent to being an NPC. Non Playable Characters were designed to assist in the game's functionality, yet those characters are not capable of leveling up or collecting memory. Thus, causing your character to remain in a perpetually looping routine without straying from the path to form a unique experience, will make them no more than a computer-generated character.

This cheat code does not mean pursuing memory badges is required daily, although it suggests completing a memory at least once every seven logins. If the character is capable and has enough energy to do more than one every seven days, go for it! There are infinite amounts of possibilities to find a memory badge daily. Often characters are invited to participate in missions to form memories although decline because of an insignificant amount of anxiety. Rather than succumbing to pesky anxiety, as long as your energy bar is willing, accept as many invites as possible.

If your character has their energy bar greater than 60% then they are capable of accepting an adventure and putting on their adventurer hat. With the adventurer hat ready to be put on, the next mission invite needs to be accepted. Overlook the avatar's initial anxiety reaction and accept the offer. A simple reminder to tell the character, assuming 60% health, "Will you remember this day one season from now." If yes, accept the adventure.

Imagine your favorite team member coming up to your character with an invite to go to a music festival. Your character has 75% energy, although is nervous about a two-day commitment. The festival has some of your character's favorite music and there are delicious restaurants around the venue. Typically your character might say no and remain at the headquarters without collecting any memory badges. Remembering the "Adventurer" cheat code, you decide to accept the invitation, put on the adventurer hat, and go! Two days from now, your character has collected numerous memories, leveled up, and made new friends.

Instead of constantly saying no to potential memory badge-generating invitations, start saying yes and enjoy reminiscing on those clips forever. It is a three-letter word but is oh-so-powerful. Next time a memory invitation contract comes across your imaginary desk, ink that document with a firm YES and go have fun!

CHEAT CODE #62: SURRENDER

Never surrender. Or never surrender in most situations. Why not all situations? Some situations can't be changed. There is no reason to dedicate your character's mental and physical energy to switch the outcome of missions incapable of editing. When our character runs into these circumstances, the only thing there is left to do is surrender. Surrender, give maximum effort, and hope for the best.

Joining missions allows Players to see their avatar's abilities, yet every mission is full of unknown possibilities. Due to this, a Player can only focus their character's energy bar on the interactive parts of the mission. The only constant in the Earth game is change. Change happens so often that the possibility of guessing is impossible. By accepting this realization, the character's energy bar will drain slower. If a character typically loses 10% energy during a mission but loses focus or feels anxious about uncontrollable segments, by properly surrendering to these possibilities the Dev team is allowing the energy reduction to happen twice as slow. In the previous example, the character would lose 5% rather than 10%. Without having sufficient energy, a character will not finish the mission, which makes this surrender technique valuable.

Surrendering can happen in numerous areas of the Earth game including missions, relationships, health, and much more. Every part of the game will always change and if your character does not think this is true, give it a couple of seasons. Surrendering to the change that will happen provides relief to a character. Hoping friends and team members will always enjoy your company will drain a character's energy because of worry. Trying to keep another character's desire to do missions together is a lost cause, but surrendering to the fact that they might not always be here to join missions is a weight off a character's shoulders. If someone wants to be your character's friend, great, if they don't…great. No reason to force friendship or force any aspect of the game that is not capable of editing.

Similar to the rest of the cheat codes that were discovered, this is easier said than done. The majority of the Earth game's outcomes are due to chance. A character can get injured during a mission at any moment, but that does not mean they should avoid missions. If your character is avoiding characters, why play the game? Surrender to all the random possibilities a character can't avoid knowingly and enjoy the ride.

CHEAT CODE #63: BOOT FROM PARTY

Have you ever run into another Player in the game that provides nothing yet drains drastic amounts of your energy? What if I told you, there's a cheat code that will get you away from those kinds of Players? It's true, and the cheat code takes some courage but is simple on paper. Numerous Players join the game and continually make it feel more difficult rather than being a beneficial user.

Let's do a quick thought experiment. Think about all the different Players you interact with or more importantly you have in-game chat parties with. Is there any Player that stands out who has been making the Earth game more difficult instead of easier? The Dev team figured this would happen and chose not to make any mods to this issue because they decided it was important for character development to include interactions with a spectrum of personalities. Choosing your character's teammates to complete missions with is part of the game's strategy. These Players that keep joining the party might be preventing a Player from completing the next mission. Time to stop getting held back by Players in your party that are bringing more anxiety and confusion than benefit. Let's walk through the cheat code.

The main purpose of this cheat code is to stop accepting invites from Players that harm your character. If your character has no other option but to interact with these Players, keep the interaction to a minimum and proceed to leave the lobby quickly. This harm can come from another Player being simply annoying, taking up time, holding your character back through laziness, or any other form of stagnation. Here's an example:

Annoying Player: "Hey! Want to join my party?"

You: "No thanks."

Simple as that! It's okay to cut Players from your game's story. This cheat code will help your character leapfrog to bigger missions. The temporary awkwardness is worth the long-term peace. Good luck with your missions in the game and don't be afraid to tell other Players the magical word of "No".

CHEAT CODE #64: SEND IT!

Want to try surfing, but aren't sure? SEND IT! Want to learn how to play basketball, but fear humiliation? SEND IT! Want to join theater, but instead of acting on stage, your stomach is acting up with butterflies? SEND IT! Numerous Players fear their character losing skill points or being insulted by trying something new, oh the irony. The fear of doing new missions is much scarier than the actual mission. Our avatars are capable of anything. Players need to trust that everything will be okay when trying something new.

The Creators of the game systematically generated fear triggers into situations that create the most growth. If this wall of concern wasn't installed into every character, then all avatars would be overly skilled, causing a shortage of low-level characters. Time for Players to realize that their characters are all capable of leveling up and reaching the leaderboard's top charts. Has your character ever had to talk in front of numerous characters? If your character followed through with the presentation, it was less brutal than expected.

Often for many characters, overcoming the fear before a mission was the predecessor that resulted in discovering a new favorite mission. Trying new missions that characters fear will bring harm are actually the moments that will reward their avatar with the most bonus points and badges.

This cheat code requires more effort and faith because it's easier said than done. Ask yourself "What mission do I want to do, but fear failure or harm?" This can be any mission: simple and quick or hard and lengthy. From going for a walk by yourself on a populated map; all the way up to joining a program to level up your character to receive an in-game job. Whatever this goal might be, you will do it! Be brave, get past that thick wall of fear, and take a leap of faith into the mission that scares you, yet will lead to numerous XP points! Today, write on a piece of paper, in the game, the goal you fear then tape it to the mirror in your character's bathroom. Write the words "You will" before your goal. For example "You will go for a walk downtown." Every time your character walks past it, read the words out loud while your character looks itself in the eyes. This will make the character feel like someone is telling them to do this task without being able to argue back at them.

Eventually, the character will become annoyed of reading it, causing the fear stats to not be activated, thus making it easy to start the goal. This cheat code is more difficult, yet powerful. Make your Player, SEND IT!

CHAPTER 13

CHEAT CODE #65: SCHEDULE IN PAIN

Comfort kills leveling up. During the most recent seasons, comfort has become a game-wide disease. With the Dev team adding free entertainment to technology devices through phones and computers, every user has a decision to make between being comforted with entertainment or working towards painful missions. This new decision tree has spawned a new low in missions completed across the Earth game. Rather than working towards accomplishing another mission to level up their character, Players are taking the easy road of short-term happiness which creates a reduction in the baseline of a character's happiness stat.

Too much of anything in the Earth game harms characters. Too much exercise will injure them. Too many friends will make weaker friendships. Too much entertainment will make a character lazy.

This cheat code explains the Admin deciding to reward those characters who can force painful experiences on their characters to grow even though choosing comfort through entertainment is an easy escape route. One of the notes on this cheat code page explains that the Admin wanted to test how many Players will be able to motivate their character to pick leveling up over comfort. Those that do decide to keep working towards goals are nearly unfairly rewarded for delaying entertainment to cause beneficial pain to their characters.

Beneficial pain makes entertainment that much more rewarding. Similar to the common realization of a character ingesting caffeine a few times a week rather than every day will make the energy bar reach higher peaks. Delaying entertainment and scheduling in missions, workouts, learning, or anything else uncomfortable to your character will make entertainment more enjoyable and increase a Player's stats by providing critical rest instead of laziness.

Characters that are not used to going for runs and tend to live stream other Players' games, go outside and take your avatar for a run, then come back and take a break with some entertainment. Now your character has finished a strength and cardio-building mission and can watch a show without guilt because sitting down will expedite the character's body recovery. Maybe your character spawned into a family that has a surplus of tokens and prevented your avatar from seeing the pain that comes with poverty. Look on the map and plan a trip to spend time in less fortunate areas, volunteer your time to help them while constantly absorbing what their daily lives are like. When your character returns to their safe, bountiful, and friendly environment, they'll appreciate the comforts and luxury significantly more.

Deciding to schedule pain into your character's life varies depending on their preconditioned life events. Start small and increase the painful/uncomfortable occurrences depending on your character's abilities. The more difficult the mission, the more the character's appreciation stat will increase. Through this contrary thinking cheat code, a character can turn their current situation into a dream life. There is always a character out there in the Earth game doing worse than yours. Perspective creates reality. If your character experiences a common life, go experience poverty, train through exercise harder, or join more missions, your character's comfortable life will feel like a dream come true.

CHEAT CODE #66: ACT EARLY

Health bar blinking red? Maybe the health bar is on a steep decline to "sick" status. Sooner rather than later: stop, lie down, and rest. No need to continue doing missions with your health bar being at 40% or lower. Once the health bar reduces by more than 20% in one day, it is time to bring keen awareness to your character's overall health. Drop all missions going on, the only mission that needs attention is battling the illness and recovering.

Characters that become infected need quick attention. Often Players will allow an avatar to continue with their missions even though the character is operating in a vastly declined state of mind. There are numerous different illnesses to contract in the Earth game. Although each sickness ranges in severity, each one is better battled by using the "Act Early" cheat code. By acting early, the Devs coded the odds to be vastly greater for a character to overcome any illness ranging from a common cold to cancer. Once there is a new pain or reduction in the health bar of some sort, completing new badges and gaining XP comes second. Without proper care, any illness can cause long-term damage or possibly the character to die.

This cheat code sounds simple, but is commonly overlooked by avatars trying to "tough it out." Even the avatars that are of the highest levels, fall prey to dying or being severely damaged from preventable illnesses. There are numerous different aspects to the game of "Earth" that can prevent diseases, but this cheat code is honing in on the importance of acting early.

Acting early comes in a few forms and we will go through the two more common ways to act early. The first way to act early for common illnesses like the flu or a cold is to stop everything your character is doing and rest. Relax, don't over-exhaust the avatar. It's time to sleep, drink fluids, and eat nutritious meals. Research other ways to properly heal from your character's exact situation, but one thing for certain is that resting will help. Do not wait to start relaxing once your character's health is already depleted. Be conscious of the health bar and start relaxing as soon as there is a discrepancy.

The second way to act early is to schedule a wellness check with an in-game doctor at least twice a season. This way, the doctor can scan the body of the character to determine if there are disturbances in the body. For instance, the doctor can look for long-term diseases, tumors, and much more. Numerous deadly diseases, if caught early, can have a higher chance of beating the disease and continuing to play the game with normal health levels.

If something is wrong with your character's health, act now! Do not wait or continue to complete missions. Without beating the illness, there will be no more missions to level up and complete. Depending on the illness, rest or go to a doctor to seek more help. Your character will always benefit from acting early.

CHEAT CODE #67: REMOVING FRIENDS

I would rather be happy than have you. Adding friends is a skill and if used correctly will increase the success rate of missions dramatically. Success rates on missions will be enhanced whether the net positive friend is currently participating or not. Keeping a healthy circle of friends gives your character stat boosts constantly, since your character will have a clear mind knowing their relationships are healthy.

Toxic "friendships" are not so much friendships at all. The constant reminder an avatar feels remembering they are on the same team as a harmful avatar hinders missions and individual stat levels. A thorn in the foot is equivalent to having a toxic friend in the group. Removing friends can be just as easy as removing a thorn in a foot and much more relieving.

The remove friend cheat code explains the step-by-step on how to remove and set healthy boundaries with other Players. It is better to not have a friend than to have a harmful friend. It is better to walk alone than to drag another along the trail. The first step to this cheat code is the realization of the thorn in the foot. In this case, the first step is to determine who is holding your character back and subtracting XP simply through acquaintance. Spending time with quality characters generates a slow, but rewarding XP boost. On the other hand, sharing valuable moments with harmful avatars mediocrely drains XP although over time has drastic effects.

Have your character pull up their friend list. Go through each username and mark next to their names a plus sign, zero, or minus sign. Plus referring to friends that provide positivity. Zero for those friends that are typically not beneficial or counterproductive. Minus sign for characters who promote a negative feeling simply by thinking of them. Once your character finishes marking the friends list with one of these symbols, it's time to do the last step to this cheat code. The friends with a plus next to their username, notice who they are and plan to do the majority of missions with them. For those friends with a zero next to their name, notice them and realize spending time with them will most likely keep your XP constant, which is beneficial since their presence is not harmful. Now for the most important part of the cheat code, find the friends with a minus sign next to their usernames. These characters you will premeditatively avoid. Avoid these usernames with no judgment and more so of an understanding that they simply are not a helpful blend for your character. Just like how oil and water do not mix. No need to force a friendship that does not work well together. Stop sending them invites, consciously keep your distance, and most critically do not speak poorly about them. Keep your thoughts to yourself and start the healing process. Have your character say independently, "I wish you happiness. I wish you to be free from suffering." Allowing your character to think this will boost their compassion levels, allowing for unforeseen byproducts of stat boosts in different categories.

We wouldn't want our character to live in a headquarters with bugs inside causing an annoyance. So why should Players spend time with other Players that provide minimal benefit, but much pain? Notice those avatars constantly bugging your character, put a minus sign by their name, then remove them as a friend. Some friends will feel like having balloons on the back, causing avatars to feel metaphorically lighter. Where spending time with harmful avatars makes our character feel weighed down. Next time your character is feeling pressure, think to yourself if this pain is from a "friend." If so, remove them and feel instantly lighter and liberated.

CHEAT CODE #68: ADAPT

With every season comes new inventions. With new inventions comes an advantage over the characters still using older versions. With early adopters starts a quickly leveling-up amount of advantage. From the beginning of the game until now this phenomenon has occurred without fail all the time.

In the early seasons, the characters that figured out how to hunt more efficiently by using tools leveled up instantly as opposed to their teammates who continued to hunt animals with their hands. Then the invention of farming developed which gave the teams adapting to using this mass food creation technique an advantage by allowing their societies to develop past constantly worrying about scavenging for food. Adapting to this newfound technology of farming gave characters the opportunity to focus on missions that developed more inventions making life easier and more dynamic.

As seasons passed the snowball of inventions never stopped. Being able to work on missions while having their hunger fulfilled, started the exponential rise to technology that would change the Earth game daily. With technology advancing continuously constantly, allowed characters to have small windows to adapt and utilize the advantages of these new tools. Characters who are hoping to level up to the near maximum level will want to incorporate this "Adapt" cheat code into their portfolio of skills.

Adapting is simple in the code of the game, yet the majority of characters are slow to adapt to new technology or knowledge until many Players are already using the new tech and instead of making an advantage for their character it simply catches them up. According to the analytics the Admin linked to this cheat code, characters are slow to adapt often because of irrational fear of change and laziness. An overwhelming number of characters have the initial stats of low acceptance to change. This means few characters are willing to use the "Adapt" cheat code to their advantage.

How do you have your character use the "Adapt" cheat code? Simple, next time there is a new technology that makes the Earth game easier, that is a moment to adapt. Cars made transporting from map to map instantly easier. In this season, being determined to buy a car to utilize its new abilities would be advantageous causing the character to level up. When the internet came out, a lot of characters refused to believe instant access to communication and knowledge would be here to stay. Then those in a position to make a business around the use of the internet made non-believers feel the pain of not adapting through missing out on token gains. As this book is being released, the newest technology Players need to have their characters adapt to is the creation of AI. This tool is as powerful as all the tools combined. Instead of requiring years of education to understand a topic, a user can talk with these AI chat interfaces for instant knowledge on any topic in the world with clarity and lack of judgment. In the future, there will be more tools to take advantage of after AI, but let's walk through an example of what adapting to AI looks like for a character.

Imagine a character named Sam. Sam has been struggling with finding a job because his resume document does not represent well the strength of Sam's skills. Sam is applying for a job as a chef in a high-end restaurant but lacks the writing skills for creating a compelling resume that will make someone want to hire him. Sam finds this "Adapt" cheat code and hears about the newest technology to adapt to AI. He looks up on his phone in the applications section "AI chat." After opening the program, he talks to the AI like it's an expert person at creating resumes. The program asks for a list of his past employment, skills, education levels, and other interesting facts. The program then creates an attractive resume for Sam to send to restaurants. To Sam's disbelief, his favorite restaurant called him after a few days after applying asking for Sam to come in and show his cooking skills. Sam received the job by showing off his skills and letting AI fill gaps in skills that he lacks.

While your character goes about playing the game. Keep an eye out for new emerging technology or knowledge that will make the game easier. Making certain parts of the game easier will allow more time to commit to other missions that feel more meaningful. Adapting to new technology will not only give an advantage over other characters but also make your character's happiness levels rise. As of now, simply try the new technology known as AI chat and see how your character levels up a lot faster.

CHEAT CODE #69: KEEP GOING

Want to complete a mission and earn a badge? Just keep going until you finish. You can't lose a mission if you never quit. Only those who forfeit lose a mission. Keep going until the mission turns the tides in your character's favor. The Earth game was designed to be around for an infinite amount of seasons whether there are still Players in the game or not, the Earth game will continue. Eventually, the Dev team expects the characters of Earth to succeed from the current season's planet and continue exploration to new planets. Characters will continually pass the baton to preserve the human character's existence. The Admin discussed leaving the outcome of Earth up to the Players of the game. They do not mind if all the human characters stop playing or not. If this were to occur, the Admin will continue to evolve new styles of intelligent characters to load into Earth for an infinite amount of seasons. This being said, there are an infinite amount of seasons to the game, so if there is a mission that you would like your character to complete, start the mission and keep going until it is completed.

But what if I do not have enough lifespan left in my character before completing a mission? The majority of missions are capable of being completed in a few seasons, although if this is the circumstance for a rare mission, fear not. All Players have the option to respawn back to the Earth game after their character's life span expires. After a character finishes their lifespan limit in the Earth game, they are removed from the game and put into the record books for eternity to be reflected back on for their accomplishments. Once this happens, a Player can simply decide to play the game again and start over. The Admin allows all Players, who helped or harmed the game, to come back and try again if they so please. All they have to do is click, play again, then be reset back to level one, zero badges, a new starting point, random character stat skills, and the ability to level up through the ranks all over again.

Knowing this, start that mission you have been hoping your character to complete, today. Stop postponing and do not quit. All characters have the ability to continue going on a mission for as long as their lifespan allows. The circumstances might change depending on the age and level of the avatar, but regardless of this, the character can always pursue missions; short-term and long-term.

If a Player is hoping for their avatar to complete a hundred-mile run in their lifespan, start training today. The character might not have the ability to finish this race after one season, two seasons, or possibly five seasons, yet do not be discouraged. This cheat code explains "Keep Going" because, at the simplest level, that is all a character needs to do to finish a mission. This scenario begins with finishing one mile, then have them try for two miles, and so on until they reach a hundred-mile run. If the character keeps trying to reach this mission's completion the Admin have developed the game in a way that helps them develop in ways that would not be realized at the beginning of the journey although will allow them to eventually accomplish their goals.

A character does not know what they do not know. If a character knew what the whole path looked like to finish a mission, it would be boring. In the same way, watching a movie for the second time is not as exciting because the surprise factor disappears. Embrace the unknown of the mission. Numerous checkpoints can not be foreseen by a character which will give them new thoughts to help with the completion of the journey. Going back to the running example, a character new to the running world will assume to lace up standard running shoes, go on a mile run and see nothing wrong with the running shoes. Once they reach a five-mile run, the character will start to think there has to be a better shoe to run in. Thinking this, the Player starts doing research on the internet for proper running techniques and better shoes to reduce knee and foot pain. After doing this research the character finds proper running shoes and better form then sets out on a five-mile run with much more ease. When the character started running for the first time, they did not know they would learn there is more to running than they realized when beginning.

Do you have a mission in mind that your character has been putting off because they are not sure they will complete the journey? Maybe your character is in the middle of a mission and wants to quit? Just keep going. Take one day at a time. The days and seasons are going to pass by regardless if your character is working towards missions or not. Might as well start and continue missions because in the blink of an eye, the game will be seasons from now. Would you rather keep going so that in a few seasons you can look back at your character's progress or do nothing and stay at your current level while time passes by? Up to you. This cheat code from the Dev team explains the importance of simply to just "Keep Going!"

EPILOGUE

I think they're on to me. The last time I was in the office I was able to find the hundredth cheat code. In order to find more cheat codes I've been needing to get a little more invasive by physically sneaking into the Admin's office and going on their computers while they're immersed in the Earth game doing quality control. The gaming experience in our world is so immersive that Players are unaware of their real life surroundings. Knowing this and knowing the trust our office has in each other, I decided this would be a critical moment if I wanted to find more cheat codes.

Unfortunately, I had a super awkward interaction with one of the Admins recently. For whatever reason they unplugged from the game suddenly. Literally, while I was on the computer right behind them. The only thing I could think of to say was "My computer died and I was in the middle of an email replying to a raging Player. I was panicking so I ran into this room and saw I could log in to my account on this computer." Their facial expression and reaction seemed to believe me, but those beings are Admin for a reason. Their level of intelligence is far superior to mine. Some other Employees joke around that the Admin and Dev team are all capable of mind reading. Let's hope not.

Until that moment, I was able to collect, translate and file sixty nine cheat codes. There are still thirty one more raw files that I still need to go through to make them comprehensible to the typical Player of the Earth game. I flew far under the radar for over a complete season while uncovering and translating the current cheat codes. Not going to lie, as of recently I've been extremely nervous about releasing these cheat codes to the entire game. I'm not sure if I'm ready for the repercussions. Since you are reading this, obviously I got over my fears.

When I first planned on rebelling against the Admin by finding the most cheat codes ever, I was going to release them with my main Earth game character then look the Admin in the eyes and accept my sentence on the chin. Now that I can only release about seventy percent of the cheat codes, I have a new plan. There's a character I control in the Earth game that was created using a VPN to hide my computer's IP address. Other beings do this when they want to explore the Earth game in secrecy. Typically Players use this tactic to have a "Bucket List Life". Going through the game with the intent to try everything the Earth game has to offer.

This is just the kind of mission that my character would love to join. He's considering publishing this book as part of one of his bucket list missions. He always wanted to write a book at a young level and now this is the perfect opportunity to fulfill that goal and level him up in the process.

By publishing this book, my character has the chance to increase his stats in nearly every category on his abilities page. Through reading, thinking, examining, and uploading this book, he'll receive a massive XP boost. Leveling up in a way that will pay dividends to his character in the form of knowledge, possibly tokens, and the release of fear to write another book.

I have yet to find a cheat code in the Admin's files titled "Write a Book", but seeing the potential XP boosts that my character will receive qualifies this mission as a cheat code. I'm not recommending writing a book that can have a deadly result to a character like this book. Although if your character wants to pursue a long-term mission that will cause them to reconsider finishing throughout the process yet provide massive amounts of XP, have them write a book.

I guess now we see what happens with the release of these confidential texts directly from the files of the Admin to the Earth game. If enough Players utilize these cheat codes, especially those characters struggling to level up, the Admin will be forced to update the code that releases the harsh restrictions placed on new Players' characters. In the meantime, I'm going to lay low for a while and finish translating the rest of these cheat codes. If the Admin doesn't figure out I was the one who leaked them, I'll push out an update to this current file in the future.

At the end of the day, remember that Earth is simply a game. One of the infinite amounts of games in existence. It might be the most popular game but does not need to be treated so seriously. Go ahead and try as many missions as possible. Turn that dream life into a reality for your character. Most importantly, make memories, build relationships and enjoy the process of leveling up your character. As I explained at the beginning of the book:

Life's a game, start playing.